D1586709

Glasgow Necropolis
AFTERLIVES
TALES OF INTERMENTS

PHOTOGRAPHED
AND COMPILED
BY
RUTH JOHNSTON

PUBLISHED BY

JOHNSTONDESIGN

First published September 2007

by Johnstondesign 4 Westercraigs Glasgow G31 2HZ

ISBN 10 0-9552284-1-7 ISBN 13 978-0-9552284-1-4

TO LIVE IN THE HEARTS OF THOSE
WE LEAVE BEHIND IS NOT TO DIE

FOREWORD

I hope you enjoy this book as much as I have enjoyed researching and compiling some of the inspiring and sad stories which relate to the monuments in the Glasgow Necropolis. From the 3,500 monuments I have selected and photographed around 150 of them, inscribed for people from all backgrounds and positions in society, some of whom became major players in the development of Glasgow during its time as the 'Second City of the Empire.' Many monuments are included purely from a personal view that they are wonderful pieces of art in their own right.

Some of the many architects and sculptors who were inspired to create some of the beautiful monuments include Alexander 'Greek' Thomson, J T Rochead, David Hamilton, John Bryce, Charles Wilson and Charles Rennie Mackintosh. Indeed Mackintosh has a particular connection to the Necropolis as he lived in a tenement in Dennistoun, on the eastern boundary of the Necropolis and his earliest commission was to design a monument here.

Every effort has been made to ensure all credits are given where due.

ACKNOWLEDGEMENTS

With thanks for their help and support

Nigel and Christine Willis

Gary Nisbet

Iain McNair

John Haxton

Paul McIntyre and Nelson Richards

Iain Allison

Margaret Greene

Elspeth King

Michael Donnelly

Lucille Furey

Dennis McCue

Alex Morrison

The Greek alphabet has 24 letters so the Merchants' House could have allocated an acre to a letter when the Necropolis first opened but it was not planned like that. By 1857, 15 of the letters had been allocated to unequal size portions and they decided not to use the monosyllabic letters but added a word which translates from the greek as monument - mnema. When the Necropolis was expanded east and south into the quarry they started using Roman divisions. The paths were used to separate section from section which leads to some strange situations of monuments very close to each other being in different sections. Some paths are now also grassed over and not obvious as divisions.

GREEK DIVISIONS	ROMAN DIVISIONS
ALPHA	PRIMUS
BETA	SECUNDUS
GAMMA	TERTIUS
DELTA	QUARTUS
EPSILON	QUINTUS
ZETA	SEXTUS
ETA	
THETA	
IOTA	
KAPPA	
LAMBDA	
MU	
NU	
I	
OMICRON	
PI	
RHO	
SIGMA	
TAU	
UPSILON	
PHI	
CHI	
PSI	
OMEGA	

MNEMA - MONUMENT

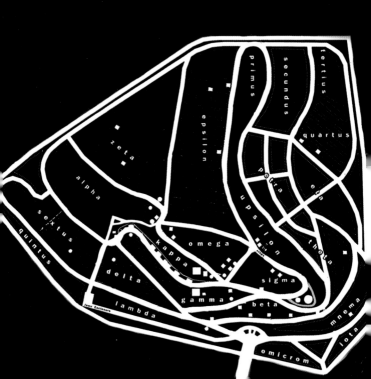

CONTENTS

FIR PARK OR MERCHANTS' PARK

In 1650 the [1] Merchants' House purchased the land, then part
of the estate of Wester Craigs, now known as the Glasgow
Necropolis. As the west side was rocky and not able to be
developed it was planted with fir trees and became known as
Fir Park. By 1804, the Scots Firs in the Park were dying, probably
due to industrialisation in the city, and they were replaced by a
mix of trees and shrubs. The area was developed into a more
formal Park and renamed Merchants' Park, (but that name wasn't
generally adopted) with carriage paths laid out and a bandstand.
The Merchants' House erected the John Knox monument in the
Park in 1825.

THE DESIGN FOR THE GLASGOW NECROPOLIS

in 1831, John Strang, historian and Chamberlain at the
Merchants' House, wrote "Necropolis Glasguensis", or "Thoughts
on Death and Moral Stimulus" and commented :-
*"The Fir Park appears admirably adapted for a Pere la Chaise, which
would harmonise beautifully with the adjacent scenery, and constitute
a solemn and appropriate appendage to the venerable structure (the
Cathedral) in front of which, while it will afford a much wanted
accommodation to the higher classes, would at the same time convert
an unproductive property into a general and lucrative source of profit,
to a charitable institution'*

The view above is from the aforementioned book and shows
'The View of the Ground for the Proposed Cemetery' with
John Knox in the background and the *Molindinar Burn flowing
between the Cathedral and the Hill. John Strang also
published many articles about his thoughts on the matter.

In 1828 a meeting, to discuss forming the Necropolis, took place
with the Lord Dean of Guild of Merchants' House, Mr Ewing, along
with Mr Dennistoun of Golfhill, Mr MacKenzie of Craigpark,
Mr Laurence Hill, the collector of the Merchants' House and
Mr Douglas of Barloch, clerk to the Merchants' House.
They all agreed to the idea and asked architect, David Hamilton,
Stuart Murray, Curator of the Botanical Gardens, and James
Clelland, Superintendent of Public Works, to produce a feasibility
study for forming the Glasgow Necropolis and a competition was
launched in 1831.

The competition for converting the Fir Park into a cemetery with
5 prizes of £10 - £50 was advertised in the press of the day.
Over in Edinburgh it was recorded that they did not think that
Glasgow had the 'sense or taste or fancy' to deliver the concept
of this garden cemetery. Sixteen plans for the Necropolis were
received and they were put on exhibition in the Dilettante
Society's (see page 121) Exhibition Rooms in Argyle Arcade.

David Bryce of Edinburgh won first prize and his brother, John
Bryce of Glasgow, came second. However, in conjunction with
architect John Baird (primus), David Hamilton was appointed to
combine the five prize winning competition designs for the
Glasgow Necropolis into one and they decided that the work
would best be undertaken by a landscape gardener. George
Mylne was selected, made Superintendent and appointed to
surpervise the work of a team of gardeners.

THE GLASGOW NECROPOLIS

The 'Bridge of Sighs' was built over the Molindinar Burn which gave an access to the Necropolis from beside the Cathedral instead of from the south. Unfortunately the Molindinar became more and more contaminated and in 1877 it was culverted.

The Necropolis was one of the few cemeteries to keep records of the dead, including profession, ages, sex and cause of death. It was also interdenominational and the first burial in 1832 was that of a Jew, Joseph Levi, a jeweller. In 1833 the first Christian burial was the stepmother of the Superintendent, George Mylne. His son, who died aged 4, unusually has a separate stone.

The costs for a lair at the top of the hill at 2 pounds and 10 shillings was double that of lower down and there were four styles of funerals to choose from costing from 2 pounds and 10 shillings down to 5 shillings plus the cost of the gravedigging and memorials. Even an unmarked common ground burial for an adult was about 4 shillings. Despite the level of costs The Glasgow Necropolis was very successful.

After 1860, the first extensions east and south took up the Ladywell quarry and in 1877 and 1892/3, the final extensions to the north and south-east were constructed, increasing the size of the The Necropolis to 37 acres (15 ha). 50,000 burials have taken place at the Necropolis and most of the 3,500 tombs have been constructed up to 14 feet deep, with stone walls and brick partitions.

There are monuments here designed by major architects and sculptors of the time, including Alexander 'Greek' Thomson, Charles Rennie Mackintosh and JT Rochead, in every architectural style, created for the prominent and wealthy entreprenuers of the 'Second City of the Empire'.

It was the first garden cemetery in Scotland but contemporary with ones in Liverpool, Dublin and London's Kensal Green. In Glasgow other garden cemeteries followed including Sighthill in 1840, the Southern Necropolis in 1840 and the Eastern Necropolis in 1847. The Roman Catholic community opened St Mary's Churchyard in Calton in 1839 and St Peter's burying ground in Dalbeth in 1851.

In 1855 The Burial Grounds (Scotland) Act led to the closure of old, crowded churchyards and burying grounds and the first of the new burying grounds on the outskirts of the city were Craigton in 1873, Cathcart in 1877, Lambhill (85acres) in 1881, the Western Necropolis in 1882 and St Kentigern's in 1882 (north west of the city). The first crematorium to be built in Scotland was Glasgow Crematorium in the grounds of the Western Necropolis in 1895.

In 1966, the Merchants' House gave the Glasgow Necropolis and £50,000 (nearly half of this sum was funds received by the Mechants' House for the upkeep of particular monuments) to the Glasgow City Council which now administers and maintains it.

In July 1878 the visitors book shows that 13,733 people visited the Glasgow Necropolis - 12,400 Glasgow citizens and 1,333 other visitors. Although the numbers are not quite at that level these days, The Glasgow Necropolis has a wonderful atmosphere and still attracts many visitors both locally and from all over the world.

*Molindinar - the word translates roughly as millrace

NOTE 1 : The Merchants' House was established in 1605 and is still active today. For over 200 years it held the majority on the Glasgow Town Council and the Lord Provosts of Glasgow were usually members of the House. It developed into one of the most important charitable institutions in Glasgow.

VICTORIAN LANGUAGE OF FLOWERS

Adonis	Sorrowful remembrance
Aloe	Grief or affection
Amaranth	Immortality
Anenome	Forsaken
Aspen Tree	Lamentation
Balm	Sympathy
Bay Tree	Glory
Carnation (red)	Alas for my poor heart
Clover 4 leaf	Be mine
Clover white	Think of me
Convolvulus major	Extinguished hopes
Cowslip	Pensiveness
Cypress	Death, despair, mourning
Daffodil	Chivalry
Daisy wild	I will think of it
Dead leaves	Sadness
Dogwood	Durability
Elm	Dignity
Flowering reed	Confidence in heaven
Forget me not	True Love
Foxglove	Insincerity
Gorse	Enduring affection
Geranium dark	Melancholy
Geranium scarlet	Comforting
Gloxinia	Proud spirit
Harebell	Grief
Hawthorn	Hope
Hemlock	You will be my death
Honeysuckle	Bonds of love
Hyacinth purple	Sorrow
Ivy	Friendship
Jasmine Carolina	Separation
Laburnum	Forsaken
Lavender	Distrust
Locust flower	Affection beyond the grave
Love lies bleeding	Hopeless
Magnolia	Dignity
Marigold	Grief despair
Moss	Maternal Love
Mulberry Tree	I shall not survive you
Nettle	You are cruel
Oats	The witching soul of music
Olive	Peace
Pansy	Thoughts
Pear Tree	Comfort
Pepermint	Warmth of feeling
Perriwinkle white	Pleasures of memory
Petunia	Never despair
Poppy oriental	Silence
Primrose	Early youth or sadness
Raspberry	Remorse
Rosemary	Remembrance
Salvia red	For ever thine
Snowdrop	Hope
Sweet Basil	Good wishes
Tulip yellow	Hopeless love
Verbena white	Pure and guileless
Veronica	Fidelity
Virginia creeper	Ever changing
Water lily	Purity of heart
White lily	Purity and modesty
Weeping Willow	Mourning
Yew	Sorrow
Zinnia	Thoughts of absent friends

3

THE NECROPOLIS GEOLOGY

Just over 300 million years ago, In the Carboniferous age, Scotland was just south of the Equator with a tropical climate.

Trees could grow to 15m or more in height in only a few years before dying and contributing to the accumulation of peat. About 15m of peat forms 1m of coal given the right conditions and around the Necropolis area, the presence of thick peat bogs and lush tropical forests is indicated by the presence of many coal seams.

10 million years later molten rock was squeezed between the layers of Carboniferous (coal bearing) sedimentary strata and cooled to form a flat-lying sheet called a sill. This molten rock, or magma, cooled and crystallised to form the rock we call dolerite or whinstone which now caps the Necropolis.

The present landscape of the Necropolis is due to glacial erosion during the ice ages of the last 2 million years. Eastward moving ice over 1 km thick with rock debris at its base acted like sandpaper, which eroded and streamlined the shape of the Necropolis as a crag. The last ice age in Glasgow receded westwards and melted about 10,500 years ago. When the ice cleared the area, the local sea level stood about 30-40m above the present day's, so the sea may have lapped along the base of the Necropolis hill which is now, at it's summit, 68m above the river Clyde.

The great mass of hard dolerite protected the underlying softer sandstone from the erosive forces of the ice so the tombs had to be blasted out of the solid rock on the brow of the Necropolis. In the valley the graves were able to be dug with the spade into the glacial deposits left by the ice and the soils developed on them.

VICTORIAN SYMBOLS OF DEATH

Anchor	A sailor or symbol of hope
Anchor and vines	Strong Christian faith
Angel	
a) flying	Resurrection
b) weeping	Grief
Ankh	Egyptian for life/immortality
Bird	Resurrection
Butterfly	Resurrection
Burning bush	Church of Scotland
Cherub	Departure of the soul
Column(broken)	Young death
Cross	
a) Celtic	Unity of heaven and earth
b) Christian	Death and resurrection
Dawn (sun)	Resurrection
Doorway	Entrance from this world to the next
Fleur de lys	Holy Trinity
Garlands	Victory over death
Grapes/vines	Sacrifice
Handshake	Farewell
Hourglass (Winged)	Life passing (time flies)
Ivy	Immortality
Lamb	
a) alone	Purity/Sacrifice
b) flag or cross	Agnus Dei (Christ's sacrifice)

5 Colin Dunlop.

GATEKEEPER'S LODGE
or CEMETERY LODGE 1839
Designed by architect David Hamilton

This building was constructed from some of the stones of the first Barony Church which stood near here. The Barony congregation had formerly used the lower church of the Cathedral.

THE SUPERINTENDENT'S HOUSE
or LODGE 1890
Designed by architect D and J Hamilton

This house was built in 1890 but the first house for the Superintendent, described as a 'swiss cottage,' was built in 1848 on an elevated piece of ground to the south of

THE BRIDGE OF SIGHS 1834
Designed by architect James Hamilton

The bridge, made from stone from Milton quarry, has 3 arches : a 60ft main arch over the river known as the Molindinar Burn which now runs underground; a second arch wide enough for horse and cart/carriage ; a

small, third arch, 'constructed from some of the oldest masonry in Glasgow', which allowed the millrace to get to the Subdean Corn Mill, near our Lady's Well (now covered by an urn) in Ladywell Street and near where the original Superintendent's lodge was.

The foundation stone of the bridge was laid in 1833 and had a time capsule buried below it. At the ceremony there was a procession led by Lord Provost James Ewing (see page 60) and then a sermon by Rev Macfarlan (see page 57) . This inscription was written by the latter and was originally on an obelisk along with the inscription which is now on the Facade.

The Necropolis or
Ornamental Public Cemetery
was constructed by
The Merchants' House of Glasgow
In their property
To supply the Accommodation required
By a rapidly-increasing population
And by embellishing the Place of Sepulture
To invest with more Soothing Associations
That Affectionate Recollection of the Departed
Which is cherished by those who survive
AD MDCCCXXXIII
Even from the tomb the voice of nature cries

Reverend Dr Black of the Barony Church (see page 63)
offered a prayer at the end of the ceremony

THE ENTRANCE FACADE 1835
Designed by architect John Bryce

The Facade was built as a retaining wall when the road was widened to allow carriages to turn round. The stone is from Kenmure quarry. A central archway is the entrance to two mausoleums and the two wings each have space for two mausoleums. All the entrances originally had cast iron gates. The bas relief is Glasgow City's coat of arms. The following inscription, written by James Hutcheson, Dean of Guild at the laying of the foundation stone of the bridge, was originally on an obelisk near here which was removed, then on the principle gate, which is missing, but is now on the facade itself as you can see in the photograph. The word adjoining was added when it was inscribed here.

> This (adjoining) Bridge
> Was erected by
> The Merchants' House of Glasgow
> To afford a proper Entrance to their new Cemetery
> Combining convenient access to the Grounds
> With suitable decoration to the venerable Cathedral
> And the surrounding scenery To unite
> The tombs of many generations who have gone before
> With The resting places destined for generations yet unborn
> Until The resurrection of the Just
> When that which is sown a Natural body
> When corruptible must put on Incrruption
> When this Mortal must put Immortality
> When death is swallowed up in Victory
> Blessed in the man who trusteth in God and whose hope the Lord is

The Facade was initially intended as an entrance to a tunnel forming a subterranean crypt running right through the hill with tiered catacombs. They were supposed 'to afford complete security against the sacrilegious burglary of the resurrectionist'.
When the Anatomy Act was passed in 1832 the idea for catacombs was abandoned. The tunnel, at present, is only a few feet deep and stores equipment.

WILLIAM MILLER 1810-1872
Sculptor John Mossman
Lambda Division

William Miller was known as the 'Laureate of the Nursery'. Born in 1810, he lived for most of his life near the Necropolis at 4 Ark Lane, Dennistoun. Miller worked as a wood turner and cabinetmaker, but was also an accomplished poet and songwriter. He is particularly remembered for the children's nursery rhyme 'Wee Willie Winkie', written for his son Stephen.

Wee Willie Winkie rins through the toon,
Up-stairs and doon-stairs in his nicht-goon,
Tirlin' at the window, cryin' at the lock,
"Are the weans in their bed, for it's now ten o'clock!"

His works were published in various magazines and also as a collection entitled Whistle-binkie: Stories for the Fireside published in 1842.

He died in 1862, poor and ill with a leg ulcer in Glasgow aged 62 and was buried in the family plot at the Tollcross Burial Ground. A monument to him was erected here by public subscription. The portrait panel is missing at present but plans are underway to reinstate it.

HUGH HAMILTON 1791-1837
Delta Division
At the cross roads of Beta, Gamma, Delta and Lambda

Hugh Hamilton was a cloth lapper in a cotton mill and he was described by contemporaries as 'a loyal subject and good citizen.'

Inscription on the south side

Erected by the Glasgow Conservative Operatives Association to the memory of Hugh Hamilton Clothlapper. Born 25th June 1791 and died 25th December 1837. 'Better is the poor that walketh in his uprightness than he that is perverse in his ways, though he be rich. Proverbs xxviii,6.

Inscription on the east side

An enlightened admirer of the British Constitution. he earned an honourable reputation amongst his fellow citizens by the grave and fervid eloquence with which he advocated our mixed form of Government.

Inscription on the west side

Sincerely attached to the Church of Scotland, he zealously defended its claims to support and extension; contended earnestly for its pure faith and simple ritual; and exemplified its precepts by a walk and conversation becoming the Gospel.

DR JACOBUS BROWN d1856
Sculptor James Fillans - white marble portrait
Beta Division

The snake wrapped round the staff is called the caduceus and is the
symbol of the medical profession and found on graves of doctors
and surgeons.

The inscription reads :
Jacobus Brown MD Obiit, MDCCCLVI., AETAT, LIV

MRS JOHN MACDONALD
Lambda Division

The top portion of this stone is now nearly totally obliterated by ivy. The other figure shown here on the right a short distance away is remarkably similar but is not attached to any monument.

JAMES ROBERTSON OF MULBERRY BANK 1790-1837
Delta Division

James Robertson and his wife Janet (Henderson) 1800-1872 are shown on this portrait panel. It is most unusual to see any images of women in the Necropolis. She died many years after him in 1872.

Their daughter Anne Robertson married Robert Blackie, youngest son of John Blackie, whose family business was the famous publishing house of Blackie and Son. Robert became a member of the Merchants' House in 1843. Anne and Robert are buried in Epsilon division of the Necropolis. There are other Blackie family memorials also in the Necropolis (see pages 98 and 99).

ENTRANCE TO THE JEWS' ENCLOSURE 1836
Designed by architect John Bryce
Stone carving by John Park
Cast iron gates by Thomas Edington
Lambda Division

This monument in stone from Stirling's quarry was inspired by Absalom's pillar, Jerusalem. There are various inscriptions on different parts of the column such as Mi Kamoka Baalim Jehovah : who among the gods is like unto Jehovah. There are also extracts from scripture and verses from Lord Byron's 'Hebrew Melodies' on the pedestal of the column.

Woolf Levy and a committee on behalf of the Jewish community purchased this portion of the Necropolis in 1832, prior to it being officially open. The first burial was of Joseph Levi, a jeweller, who died of dysentry in 1832. There are 16 interments within the enclosure and two outside it against the south wall. One of those was through a disagreement in the Synagogue and the other through Morris Isaac Reubens having married a 'Christian woman'.

The Jewish faith does not allow more than one interment per grave so the enclosure was soon full. The Merchants' House could not come to an agreement regarding additional space within the Necropolis so subsequently the Jewish community purchased space within the Eastern Necropolis which opened in 1847.

Near here is a pit which was dug to inter hundreds of people who had died during an outbreak of cholera in 1932.

15

JOHN GRAHAM GILBERT 1794-1866
Designed by architect C H Wilson
(not to be confused with architect Charles Wilson)
Sculptor William Brodie
Delta Division

John Graham (Gilbert) was the son of a Glasgow merchant and was born in Stockwell Street, Glasgow. His father insisted that he should study to become an accountant but he abandoned that and pursued his artistic career. In 1818 he enrolled as a student at the Royal Academy in London, winning the Gold Medal for historical painting in oil.

He lived in Italy before moving to Edinburgh in 1827 and was admitted to the Scottish Academy in 1829. During his time in Edinburgh he contributed 58 pictures, 39 portraits and 19 "fancy figures", to the Academy Exhibition.

Following marriage to Jane Gilbert and taking his wife's family name in 1834, he returned to Glasgow. Seven years later he became President of the newly formed West of Scotland Academy. His studio was in Yorkhill, where his reputation was established as a portrait painter and colourist. He was a very modest man but he painted some of the most famous Glaswegians of his time and he died in 1866 aged 72.

When his widow died in 1877 his collection was left to the City of Glasgow including 77 old masters one of which is Rembrant's 'Man in Armour' now on view in Kelvingrove Art Gallery.

**ROBERT SIMPSON 1800-1887
AND HIS WIFE ELIZA (CRAIG) d1867**

THOMAS GILDARD 1822-1895
Designed by R J Gildard
Bronze Portrait Panel by William Shireffs
Sculptor Peter Smith
Sextus Division

His monument was unveiled on the first anniversary of his death.

Thomas Gildard was born in Luss in 1822 and was for five years an apprentice in architect David Hamilton's practice along with pupils, J T Rochead and Charles Wilson. On completion of his apprenticeship he set up in business with his brother-in-law, Robert Macfarlane, until Macfarlane's death in 1862.

Together they designed part of Belgrave Terrace off Great Western Road and The Britannia Music Hall in Argyle Street where Stan Laurel and Cary Grant started their careers. Gildard continued to practice until 1869 when he joined John Carrick who was Glasgow's first City Architect from 1862-89.

He regularly contributed articles to the Weekly Citizen and his reminiscences of Glasgow's architectural practices in the early 1800s were serialised in The Builder's Journal, in 1895. His nickname was Buffalo Bill due to his resemblance to that famous showman who visited Glasgow in the late 1890s. His recollections of Mossman were published in the Proceedings of the Philosophical Society of Glasgow, 1890-92. and 'An Old Glasgow Architect on some Older Ones' was published in Proceedings of the Philosophical Society of Glasgow in 1895. He died in 1895 aged 73.

CORLINDA LEE d1900
Sculptor Robert Gray
Sextus Division

This monument is to Corlinda Lee, Queen of the Gypsies. There should have been another portrait of a woman here but the bronze panel of her is missing.

She married George Smith, who belonged to one of the famous Gypsy families and they were together King and Queen of the Gypsies. They travelled widely and Queen Victoria met and had tea with them. They lived for some time in City Road, Glasgow.

The inscription on the memorial reads:

Her love for her children was great,
and she was charitable to the poor.
Wherever she pitched her tent,
she was loved and respected by all.

Erected in Loving Memory
By her Husband and family

She was laid to rest here in 1900

MARY ANNE LOCKHART 1798-1842
Designed by architect J Wallace
Sculptor J Mossman
Delta Division

It is one of many Gothic monuments in the Necropolis and it was worked on by both John Mossman and his brother William. Both were involved with the stone carving and when nearing completion of the monument William, in a letter to the third brother George, mentioned their satisfaction with the angels and how it would be one of the most impressive monuments in the Necropolis.

Robert and Thomas Lockhart were clothiers in Glasgow. Robert Lockhart, who died in 1886, employed his brother-in-law, architect J Wallace of London, to design this monument to his wife Mary Anne (Wallace) Lockhart. It was described as follows:

'The lower half of the monument is chaste, simple and massive. In the upper half it divides into an open arch and is adorned with most elaborate sculpture terminating in slender pinnacles with all the usual accompaments of crocket and finial. The various inscriptions are all in black letter, figured on scrolls and supported by winged cherubs.'

JAMES MACKENZIE OF CRAIGPARK
1760-1838
Delta Division

Genuine Egyptian style Obelisk coming straight out of the ground without a pedestal base. The only ornamental work on the south face is a burning bush in high relief. Over the burning bush is the motto 'Luceo non uro' which is the MacKenzie clan motto and translates as 'I shine, not burn'. Also used is the Gaelic motto "Cuidich 'n righ" (Help the king)

James MacKenzie was one of the group who attended the meeting in 1828, to talk about creating the Necropolis as mentioned in the introduction.

Born in 1760 in Glasgow, he was well educated and became a well known merchant and public figure. In 1798 he bought the land of Craigpark which is now part of Dennistoun, Glasgow, and built his home, described as a 'building of some architectural pretensions'. He was Lord Provost of Glasgow 1806-07 and Provost MacKenzie was the first person in Glasgow who adopted the modern pronounciation of the name of MacKenzie instead of M'Kingie or MacKeengie. In 1805 he married Louisa Balfour, by whom he had a family of nine children, five of whom died young. He himself died in 1838 aged 77 and is buried in the crypt of Glasgow Cathedral.

The inscription on the west face of the stone is for five children of this family.
John d1812
James d1814
James d1817
Jane d1824
Louisa d1826
All died under the age of 15.

21

IN LOVING MEMO...
PETER SMITH SCULPTOR
WHO DIED 24TH MAY 1911, A... 58 YEARS.
MARGARET NICOL, HIS ...
WHO DIED 9TH AU...
JAMES NICOL SMITH, ...IR ELDEST SON
WHO DIED ... JUL... 1941, AGE... 7 YEARS.
...LLEN POLLOCK, HIS ...IFE
WHO DIED 3RD ... 1948, A... 75 YEA...
PETER, ...R ELDER SON
WHO ...ED 8TH NOVE...BER 1921, AGED 2... Y...RS.
H...EN, THE... YOU...GER DAU...TER
WHO D...D 9TH ...AY 1988, A... ... Y...R...

PETER SMITH 1843-1911
Sextus Division

He was born in Morayshire in 1843. In 1878 he set
up his own business as a monumental sculptor and
purchased the company, J & G Mossman, in 1891 soon
after John Mossman's death. (The Mossman family
monument is in Sighthill Cemetery.)

He kept the Mossman company name which is on many
monuments in the Glasgow Necropolis but also used his
own name on some of them.

The company of J & G Mossman, as well as creating
monuments for the Necropolis, had commissions
throughout Scotland and America.

His Glasgow Necropolis work includes the stonework
for the Alexander McCall Monument, designed by
Charles Rennie Mackintosh and the monument to
architect, Thomas Gildard. He produced a very large
number of Celtic crosses for the Necropolis especially in
the Zeta and Epsilon divisions with a variety of designs
by major Glasgow architects.

You will also notice a lot more monuments in the
Necropolis that look like his own.

HUGH COGAN 1757-1855
Designed by architect J T Rochead
Kappa Division

Hugh Cogan, of the company Cogan and *Bartholomew,
was Dean of Guild at the Merchants' House between
1842 and 1844. He founded the first Glasgow Building
Society and was an elder of the Free Church. His wife
was Elizabeth Orr who died the year after he did,
aged 71.

His obituary stated ' Full as his head and hands were
with what belonged to him as one of the leading
merchants and manufacturers of the city he contrived
to find time for lending zealous and effective aid to
many of our most important local institutions. As treasurer of the Infirmary, he took a lively interest in all its
affairs. In the course of an active, useful and honourable
life there is hardly one, indeed, of our educational and
benevolent institutions that that was not largely indebted to him for aid in the direction of its affairs.'

*There is a description in 1857 of a proposed monument to the
Bartholomew Family near here on a raised plot of ground marked
only by a Rowan tree.

REV ALEXANDER OGILVIE BEATTIE
1783-1858
Designed by Alexander "Greek" Thomson
Sculptor J Mossman.
Kappa Division

The monument consists of an obelisk and urn, with a tomb chest on a base. Beattie's congregation raised the money for both this monument and the one for GM Middleton (see page 70).

Rev Beattie settled into the new United Secession Church in Gordon Street, Glasgow, in 1825. His preaching attracted people from all over Glasgow, and filled the church which had a capacity of 1500.

In 1833 he studied and obtained a degree in medicine which enabled him to treat those in his congregation who could not afford to pay for medical care. At his jubilee, celebrating 50 years as a preacher, he said: 'I here, this evening, stand before you, a man who never had one hour's illness. I know not, at this moment, what it is to have a sore head. I never had one.' However, at the age of 72 he felt he had to get someone to share the work load and Rev. George Marshall

Middleton of Kinross eventually accepted in 1855. Rev Beattie will also be remembered for instigating the building of the St Vincent St Church, designed by 'Greek' Thomson and the foundation stone for that church was laid in May 1857. Unfortunately Beattie died a year later in 1858 aged 75 and Rev GM Middleton was the first to

JOHN ADAM OF LARCHGROVE
1800-1874
Kappa Division

This monument resembles a stone door with an enclosure in front. John Adam is buried in a vault in the rock under the path in front of the door. The door symbolises the way through to the next world.

John Adam was the owner of a brick, tile and pottery works at 206 Duke Street, Glasgow which was next to the cattle market and is now demolished. The Pottery was a redware one, sometimes known as brownware, making quite coarse pottery for the lower end of the market. Annfield Pottery was also near here.

He married Georgina McCritchie who died in 1886 aged 76. Larchgrove was an estate he bought when he retired and his son took over the business - there is a mansion that was converted into a remand home called Larchgrove in the Greenfield area of Glasgow off Edinburgh Road, which I believe is the site of his estate where he died in 1874 aged 74.

ROBERT BLACK MAUSOLEUM
Kappa Division

This was the first Mausoleum to be erected in the
cemetery. Robert Black, merchant, of Black & Wingate,
and owner of the cotton mills at Sandyford Street, in
Kelvinhaugh, built this for his daughter Catherine, who
died aged twelve. Five of his daughters died before they
reached the age of twenty one. He died in 1879 at the
age of 86.

Black's residence was *Glenarbuck House situated in
Old Kilpatrick, ten miles from Glasgow and is a large,
Regency style, now 'B' listed mansion.

A relation, William George Black, was senior partner in
the legal firm of Black, Honeyman, & Monteath and was
born in Glasgow in 1857. Many Black family portraits
were exhibited at the Old Glasgow Exhibition of 1894.

His grand-uncle founded the firm of Black & Wingate,
and his father's cousin the firm of James, Black & Co.
He was educated at Glasgow Academy and Glasgow
University where he won many prizes. He travelled
around the world and wrote a considerable number of
published books and articles. In 1886, in conjunction
with Mrs. Parker Smith, he formed the Women's Liberal
Unionist Association. He married in 1899 Miss Anna
Robertson Blackie, daughter of Robert Blackie, of
Blackie & Son, and Anne Robertson (see pages 98
and 14).

*The lands of Glenarbuck were acquired by Gilbert Hamilton, Provost of
Glasgow in 1792 and Dean of Guild before that. The house and gardens
were laid out and planned by him.

WILLIAM DICK MONUMENT
Fluted column

WILLIAM SLOAN MONUMENT
Vase on top
Gamma Division

WILLIAM MOTHERWELL 1797-1835
Designed by Sculptor James Fillans
Gamma Division

The small temple had a bust in white marble under the canopy. In 1878 it was described in a letter to the Glasgow Herald complaining about the condition of the monument as 'Black as an Ethiopian - covered all over with layers of soot.'

The inscription on the west face is by his friend and poet William Kennedy who, prior to there being a monument here to Motherwell's memory, visited this burial plot and placed poetry here.

Erected By admirers of the Poetic genius of WILLIAM MOTHERWELL
Who Died 1st November 1835 aged 38 years

Not as a record he lacketh a stone!
'Tis a fond debt to the singer we've known -
Proof that our love for his name hath not flown
With the frame perishing
That we are cherishing
Feelings akin to the lost poet's own

The monument has some fine friezes carved by Fillans on the other three faces which are badly weathered. The one facing the path on the east face represents 'Chivalry' the one on the north face represents a passage from Motherwell's poem 'Halbert the Grim'

The hardest may soften, the fiercest repent,
The heart of grim Halbert may never relent.

and the one on the south face represents the poet himself and his 'Jeannie Morrison' seated side by side on 'a broomy brae o' June'. He wrote his first poem to her when he was 8.

Motherwell was the son of an ironmonger and became Sheriff-Clerk Depute in Paisley. As well as writing poetry he was also the editor of a number of publications : Paisley Advertiser (1828); Glasgow Courier (1830); and author of several acclaimed books. He died suddenly in 1835.

DR JAMES JEFFRAY OF CARDOWAN
1759-1848
Gamma Division

This eminent Professor of Anatomy at Glasgow University, is buried here with his wife Margaret (Lockhart) and two sons, James, also a doctor and John, a writer. According to a story by Peter MacKenzie (see page 44), an investigative journalist of the time, Jeffray performed an experiment on a criminal who had been hung and brought him back to life. The story is related below.

Mathew Clydesdale in a drunken rage beat 80 year old Alexander Love to death in 1818. He was tried, found guilty and sentenced to hang. The sentence stated that afterwards he should be given up to Dr James Jeffray, Professor of Anatomy at Glasgow University to be dissected and anatomized. The prisoner attempted suicide by slashing his arms but the authorities managed to save him for the hangman. After the hanging the body was delivered to Dr Jeffray, placed on a chair and experiments began. The body was treated with electric shocks, came back to life and was, allegedly, finally killed by a scalpel being plunged into his neck.

Dr Ure, Jeffray's assistant, noted that that the murderer's neck wasn't dislocated and the face looked natural. However, In a paper published in 1819, he suggested that if they hadn't cut into and wounded the spinal marrow and blood vessels in the neck, draining the body of blood, and if they had 'electrified' the phrenic nerve when the body first arrived 'there is a probability that life might have been restored.' As it was, the experiment had the dead man's face and limbs twitch and move but stop as soon as the battery was disconnected.

JOHN KING OF LEVERNHOLME MAUSOLEUM
Kappa Division

An imposing family vault with polished Peterhead granite columns and cast iron gates.

Born in Stirling, King initially worked in the counting-house at the Hurlet and Campsie Alum Company near Barrhead. In 1825 he moved to Glasgow, to take over the management and became a partner in the *Cudbear Works at Dunchattan, off Duke Street, which belonged to George Macintosh. By 1848 he was running both companies.

He married Christina MacNie in 1826 and from 1841 they lived at Levernholme, in the south of Glasgow. He was a director of the Merchants' House and of the Chamber of Commerce, as well as of the Clydesdale Bank, the Forth and Clyde Navigation and the Glasgow and South-Western Railway Company. He died at Levernholme in 1875.

The mausoleum also commemorates his wife Christina McNie, his daughter Jessie Callendar King, his son Robert King of Levernholme, convenor of the County of Renfrew and Dean of Guild of Glasgow, and a grandchild.

*Cudbear - a red dying powder made from lichens.

BUCHANANS OF BELLFIELD MAUSOLEUM
Designed bv architect J Stephen
Sculptors J & G Mossman
Kappa Division

This mausoleum was built for three sisters, Margaret, Jane and Elizabeth, the Misses Buchanan of Bellfield, daughters of *George Buchanan of Woodlands, Ayrshire. The sisters lived beyond Witch Knowe in Bellfield House on the Bellfield estate near Kilmarnock. The house was described as being 'concealed by belts of trees which surround the beautiful garden and fine pleasure grounds.

Jane and Margaret both died before Elizabeth who died in April 1875. They left a large sum of money in a joint Will, changed only by one codicil by Elizabeth after her sisters' deaths, and it specifies a long list of charitable uses, 'the whole residue of the estate, after providing for these purposes, is to be paid, one half to the Glasgow Royal Infirmary and the other half to the Glasgow Asylum for the Blind.' £10,000 was also left to the Merchants' House for the perpetual upkeep of their tomb.

*George Buchanan, was one of seven brothers, five of whom were involved in the cotton trade. Intially only John (Buchanan of Carston), Walter and James were co-partners and described as "English merchants and dealers in cotton twist, wareroom, Oswald's Closs, east side, Stockwell". Later both George (Buchanan of Woodlands) and Archibald (Buchanan of Catrine) were also involved. John, the eldest brother, was a friend of the famous Richard Arkwright', textile industrialist and inventor of power-driven machinery, and was his first agent in Scotland. He sent Archibald, the youngest brother, as an apprentice to Arkwright's works at Cromford. Archibald was highly thought of by Arkwright and was well taught by him later bringing home with him an exceptional knowledge of the trade to share with his brothers.

HUTCHISON MAUSOLEUM
Kappa Division

An imposing massive tomb distinguished by the wonderful iron gates with a Moorish motif and elaborate workmanship which are now in very bad condition. It commemorates the Hutchison family of Messrs Hutchison, manufacturers, in *Hutcheson Street, Glasgow.

I am still trying to find out more information about this mausoleum and the people buried here.

*HUTCHESON STREET - Opened in 1790, occupies the site of the first Hutchesons' Hospital founded by GEORGE 1558-1639 and THOMAS HUTCHESON 1590-1641 who were both lawyers. Their father, also Thomas Hutcheson (of Lambhill) had died when Thomas was only five years old, leaving the older George to act as his guardian. Thomas received a good education and is said to have stated that this was one of "the blessings, and the pious and memorable exampell for which, under God, I am indebted to my brother George".

They endowed Hutchesons' Hospital, built in 1641-1660 on Trongate as a hospice for 12 "poore aiget decrippit men". The Hospice stood in Argyle St until 1820's and its replacement still stands in Ingram Street. The Hutcheson bothers also endowed Hutchesons' Grammar School for orphaned and under-privileged boys, which was originally housed in the Hospital building. George's office and house were on the north side of Trongate Street, near the site of the Tontine. In 1611 he built a house in Partick on the banks of the Kelvin.

They are buried in the old Cathedral Graveyard on the right hand side of the

MAUSOLEUM

...uilt for Angus Turner, Town Clerk of ...o years but he was born in Edinburgh ...rently disliked and persuaded to retire ...n of £2,500. He acted as clerk and ...es of the Clyde Navigation, the Port-Glasgow Harbour, the Clyde Lighthouses, the Bridges Trust, and the Court Houses. He died in 1876 aged 75.

His sister, Margaret Turner, married William Connel, a partner in the Cunard Line of steamers and Dean of Guild of the Merchants' House 1851-52.

There is a small recess just beyond Mr Turner's monument in which there are 3 small monuments inscribed only with initials believed to be the burying ground of
DAVID BELL
of Glasgow.

EGYPTIAN VAULTS 1837
Designed by architect David Hamilton
Cast iron gates by Thomas Edington
Kappa Division

The gates were designed with three crossed pairs of torches, inverted but not extinguished and above, on the stonework, a winged hour-glass.

These vaults were built at considerable expense by the Merchants' House to house bodies while graves were being prepared. In the case of a sudden death there was not enough time to prepare an appropriate burial ground. Before it was built, the Facade was sometimes used for this purpose.

The following is a contemporary description of the inside:

'the massive stone lids of the temporary tombs with iron rings attached are visible within, extending to the further extremity of the cavern from which they retire right and left into the excavated chambers or aisles on both sides.'

MARGARET MACNEE 1810-1847
Sigma Division

This memorial is to the wife of the famous artist Sir Daniel MacNee FRSA but other family names are also inscribed on it.

Sir Daniel MacNee was born in 1808 in Fintry, Stirlingshire and trained with artist John Knox. He was a portrait painter in Glasgow becoming an associate of the Royal Scottish Academy in 1830 and eventually becoming the President of the RSA in 1876. He was knighted in 1877, died in Edinburgh in 1882 and is buried in Dean Cemetery, Edinburgh. His wife, Margaret, died in 1847 at the age of 37.

HENRY MONTEITH OF CARSTAIRS
1765-1848
Designed by architect C H Wilson (Not to be confused with architect Charles Wilson)
Sculptor Mossman
Gamma Division

The monument is Peterhead granite and the base is Limestone.

Inscribed West side
To Henry Monteith of Carstairs Dedicated in grateful affection by his son

Inscribed East side
Henry Monteith of Carstairs Died AD 1848 aged 83 years
Respected Beloved Lamented

James senior, father of the Henry commemorated here, was apprenticed as a weaver eventually becoming a master weaver and then a manufacturer. He had six sons and the second son, James junior, was *David Dale's partner in the Blantyre cotton mill the first of which was built in 1785. Monteith and Co built a model village with a church for the workers and a schoolteacher and minister were paid for by the company. A second mill and a dyeworks was also built about six years later. He also bought the Barrowfield Dyeworks in Bridgeton, Glasgow, from Pierre Papillon, the man who brought the secret of the Turkey-red dye for bright red Bandanna handkerchiefs from Rouen.

The man commemorated here is Henry who inherited the family business when his brother, James junior, died. With the development of steam power, he was able to concentrate not only on a dyeworks but also on cotton spinning in the Bridgeton area of Glasgow. He was Lord Provost of Glasgow 1814-15 and was returned to parliament in 1821. He bought the estate of Carstairs in 1819 and he died aged 83 in 1848 but is not buried here.

CARSTAIRS STREET - was named for estate of Henry Monteith.
MONTEITH ROW AND STREET - In 1819 permission was granted for a terrace to front Glasgow Green and a street nearby to be named in honour of Henry Monteith, at that time Provost of Glasgow. John Mathieson, the manager of Henry Monteith & Co., built the first tenement in the Row.

*DAVID DALE OF ROSEDALE 1739-1806

He was the son of a grocer and born in Stewarton, Ayrshire. He began his working life as a herdboy to a local farmer, served an apprenticeship as a weaver in Paisley and afterwards moved to Hamilton where he worked as a journeyman weaver.

He then took to traveling, buying homespun linen and this work eventually evolved, in 1763, into a business in a small shop in the High Street, Glasgow, dealing in French and Dutch yarns. In 1777 he married Anne Campbell, the daughter of a director of the Royal Bank of Scotland in Edinburgh and became the Glasgow agent for the Bank in 1783, opening the Bank's first Glasgow branch. They lived in Charlotte Street, Glasgow in a house designed by Robert Adam. His brief partnership with Richard Arkwright, the cotton industrialist, which exploited Arkwright's new technology, failed mainly because Arkwright had not secured the patents on the design of the spinning frame and Dale decided to build his own cotton mill in New Lanark without paying his partner. By the 1790s the New Lanark Mills were the biggest cotton-spinning complex in Britain, employing 2,000 workers, including 400 to 500 children between the ages of 5 and 8 years who worked 13 hours a day and who were paupers from the workhouses of Glasgow and Edinburgh. He did provide his workers with an education and was perceived to be a philanphropist in his day. Further mills were built at Blantyre, Sutherland and Oban. He became a magistrate in Glasgow and was known as the 'benevolent bailie'.

Dale's daughter, Caroline Dale, married Welshman, Robert Owen in 1799. With the financial support of several businessmen from Manchester, Owen purchased Dale's textile mills in New Lanark for £60,000. Owen adopted regulations to put an end to a system which had children working for long hours at a very early age. He was influencial in the establishment of the co-operative movement and at New Lanark, he continued and expanded Dale's ideas.

Dale retired to "Rosebank" near Cambuslang, but kept on his house in Charlotte Street where he died in 1806. He was buried in the Ramshorn graveyard in the south east corner and he has the simple inscription 'David Dale, Merchant'.

REVEREND DR RALPH WARDLAW
1779-1853
Gamma Division

The monument was erected a few years after his death by his congregation. On his maternal side he was ninth in descent from James V of Scotland and a cousin of James Ewing of Strathleven (see page 60).

He was born at Dalkeith, Mid-Lothian in 1779 but his parents moved to Glasgow when he was six months old. By the age of 16 he had completed his studies at Glasgow University and he became an independent minister and an itinerant preacher. After spending some time in Perth he was offered a position there. However friends in Glasgow offered to build a chapel for him which was erected in North Albion Street and at the age of 24 he was ordained as it's pastor. That same year he married Jane Smith and they had a family of eleven children.

His sermons were evangelical, highly intellectual and very popular and a much larger chapel in West George Street was built for him.

In those controversial times he was one of Scotland's most fervent anti-slavery campaigners, and gave his Church as a meeting place for its supporters. He was prominent in Britain and America as an author on theological questions and published various theological writings.

He was appreciated as a minister and friend by his own congregation and by the members of other denominations. On his death at the age of 74 in the year of his jubilee in 1853, huge numbers of people attended his funeral including the Lord Provost, Magistrates, most of the Ministers of the city and the Professors of the University

THOMAS THOMSON 1773-1852
Sigma Division

Thomas Thomson was a famous Scottish chemist. Born in Crieff, Perthshire in 1773 he studied classics, mathematics and natural philosophy at St. Andrews University, received a medical degree from Edinburgh University in 1799 but was inspired by Joseph Black to take up chemistry.

At the age of 23, he succeeded his brother James as editor of the Supplement to the Third Edition of the Encyclopædia Britannica, contributing articles on Chemistry, Mineralogy, and Vegetable, Animal and Dyeing substances.

In 1820, these articles were the basis of his book 'System of Chemistry' using the idea of symbols. This book was translated into various languages and the system was adopted throughout the world.

He also acted as a consultant to the Scottish excise board and invented the instrument known as Allan's saccharometer - a hydrometer that measures the amount of sugar in wine and beer.

He was part of the group that founded the Wernerian Natural History Society of Edinburgh in 1808 for the purpose of promoting the study of the Sciences and of Natural History. The society remained in existence for almost 50 years.

At the age of 44 he became regius professor of Chemistry at Glasgow University, and 3 years later, he identified a new zeolite mineral, which was named Thomsonite in his honour.

ELIZA JANE AIKMAN 1852-1929
Sigma Division

She was born in Edinburgh in 1852. Her father, the
Reverend John Logan Aikman, was appointed to a church
in Anderston when she was 4 years old. He was devoted
to philanthropic causes and his name is also on this
monument on the west face.

Eliza followed his example and her knowledge of the social
conditions in Anderston at that time gave her an under-
standing of the problems facing working class families.
As a Probationary Officer for Cranstonhill she laid the
foundations of care work. In 1895 she became a member
of the 'Children's Committee of the Glasgow Parish
Council' and was involved with the care of orphans and
deserted children. She was the inspiration behind the
'Glasgow Infant Health Visitor Association', or the 'Green
Ladies' as they became known.

In 1927 she was presented by *The Trades House with a
Burgess Ticket which stated 'Miss Aikman having paid her
freedom has been admitted a Burgess and Guild Sister of
the Burgh qua Weaver, and accordingly entitled to all the
civil rights and privileges by law belonging to a free citizen'. She died in 1929 at the age of 77.

* The Trades House and the Merchants' House were both formed in 1605.
The Guilds and Craft Incorporations are the Scottish equivalent of craft
guilds formed in many European cities in the Middle Ages and The Trades
House is still in existence today. Although its political and legal functions
have been transferred to other bodies the charitable functions and concern
for the future of Glasgow remain. The encouragement of youth and support
for education, particularly the Schools and the Further Education Colleges
in developing craft standards, are now its main concerns.

JOHN TAIT d1838
Sigma Division

This is a strange stone dark brown in colour and mottled. It originally had gilt letters. The monument is the only one that I know of made from the dolerite rock on which it stands.

There is another JOHN TAIT buried nearby who does not have a memorial and is buried to the east of the Dugald Moore monument (see page 53)

THE OTHER JOHN TAIT 1795-1836
Omega Division

This 'Fearless champion of the working classes' was born of 'respectable working people' in Ayrshire who moved to Bridgeton, Glasgow, when he was six. His education was limited and at nine he was apprenticed to a weaver in Bathgate where he worked both as a weaver and farm labourer. On completion of his apprenticeship he moved to Milngavie where he met a man from Martinique who persuaded him to become a soldier. He participated in the *Battle of the Serpentine in Hyde Park in 1814 which was a re-enactment of the battle of Trafalgar. When he was discharged from the army he returned to Glasgow, weaving and married life. He then became a clerk (to Mr Wingate, an engineer) and a renowned political reformer contributing to various publications and eventually the Editor of the 'Liberator'. He died aged forty one and many people attended his funeral. A great sum of money was collected by subscription to cover his funeral, stone memorial and his family subsistence. However it was invested in an Insurance swindle and never recovered. He was buried near Dugald Moore (see page 53) but there is no monument.

*A great Fair was held in Hyde Park and three foot long scale replicas of war ships were manoeuvered about the lake in an representation of the events providing a bird's-eye-view of the battle, which had taken place in 1805. French ships sunk in flames while the National Anthem was played. Ornamental booths and taverns, provided the public with refreshments. Military bands, acrobats and roundabouts provided entertainment.

WILLIAM McGAVIN 1773-1832
Designed by architect David Bryce
Sculptor Robert Forest
(sculptor of the John Knox statue)
Sigma Division

This 35ft high Monument was erected by public subscription to commemorate William McGavin, a radical, protestant preacher.

The third son of James McGavin, a tenant farmer in Ayrshire. He went to school at the age of six until he could read the bible and then worked on the farm looking after the cattle. His father sold up and moved to Paisley when he was ten and he was apprenticed to a weaver. At the age of seventeen he began work for a bookseller. Three years later he took over teaching at a school his brother had set up and where he met his future wife, Isabella Campbell. They married seven years later when he moved to Glasgow to work as a clerk and book-keeper.

He formed an association with an independent congregation eventually becoming a well known preacher. He is particularly famous for his publication 'The Protestant' which evolved from a series of letters in The Glasgow Chronicle in May 1818 but eventually extended to several printed volumes. In a fanatical religious manner it attacked the 'errors of Popery'. It was said that it was this work that persuaded the Merchants' House to erect the John Knox Monument and that he was successfully sued for libel by the Catholic Church in 1821.

He died suddenly of apoplexy in 1832 and was buried in the crypt of Wellington St Chapel. When it was demolished he was re-interred here.

LIEUTENANT JOSEPH GOMOSZYNSKI 1813-1845
Sculptor William Mossman I
Sigma Division

This Polish exile died in Greenock in 1845 aged thirty two. He would have been about seventeen years old at the time of The November Uprising which was an armed Polish rebellion against Russia's rule in Poland. It was started in 1830 in Warsaw by a group from the Army's Officer School and supported by a large part of Polish society.

Despite some successes, the Uprising was eventually defeated in 1831 by a numerically superior Russian army. The Russian writer, General Puzyrevsky, maintained that in spite of the inequality of resources (Russia had sent over 180,000 well trained men against Poland's 70,000, 30% of whom were fresh recruits) of the two countries, Poland could have held her own against Russia. "Instead, the war lasted eight months, with often doubtful success. At times the balance seemed to tip decidedly to the side of the weaker adversary who dealt not only blows, but even ventured daring offensives."

The Scottish poet Thomas Campbell 1777–1844, whose house was in High Street, Glasgow, (a plaque commemorating him is on a wall facing the south elevation of the College Bar) championed the cause of the Poles in his poem 'The Pleasures of Hope'. He was so personally affected by the news of the capture of Warsaw by the Russians in 1831 that he wrote 'Poland preys on my heart night and day.' His sympathy found expression in the foundation of the Association of the Friends of Poland.

PETER MACKENZIE 1798-1875
Sigma Division

Peter MacKenzie was an investigative journalist in the 19th century and many of his stories are related in 'Reminiscences of Glasgow' which he published in 1865 at the age of 67.

One particular story of his, exposed fraudulent use of funds paid to a grain merchant in 1847 for famine relief of the Highlands of Scotland during this difficult time.

The evidence gained by MacKenzie was that some of the grain was adulterated and the grain merchant, Alexander Bannatyne, was brought to trial, convicted, sentenced to four months in jail and fined £400. But the man had influential friends and he was released, the fine waived and he was even paid for the grain that had been mixed with sawdust.

In the same year Mackenzie organised soup kitchens in Glasgow when there was an outbreak of typhus and starvation was rife in the city.

Another story relates to the Anatomy department of Professor James Jeffray (see page 29) which received bodies after hangings. He was an eye witness at the event in 1818 but only nineteen years old at the time and his account conflicts with the doctors notes. However, it makes for some colourful reading.

IN MEMORY OF
WALTER CRUM OF THORNLIEBANK RENFREWSHIRE
WHO DIED 4 MAY 1867 AGED 70
AND OF HIS CHILDREN WALTER EWING BORN 15 NOV. DIED ... 1837
JANE EWING BORN 2 OCT. 1829 DIED 18 JUNE 1840 JOHN BO...
DIED 21 MAY 1845 AGNES POLLOK BORN 30 JULY 1841 DIED ...
WALTER EWING WHO D... IN CALCUTTA 9 JAN. ...

HUMPHRY EWING CRUM EWING JUN
DIED AT
BETTER HOPE ESTATE, DEMERARA
MARCH 12TH 1878
AND WAS BURIED HERE
JANET CREELMAN ROBSON
HIS WIFE
DIED JUNE 14TH 1893

WALTER CRUM OF THORNLIEBANK
1796-1867
Beta Division

Walter Crum's father, Alexander Crum, along with James Crum his brother, ran a cotton manufacturing business in Thornliebank and most of the inhabitants of the village were employed there in every process from the spinning of the raw material to the finishing of the dyed and printed fabrics. Alexander was also a partner in the Merchants Bank. His wife, was the youngest daughter of Walter Ewing (Maclae) and Margaret Fisher.

Walter Crum was born in Glasgow in 1796 and he was educated at a private school, then at Glasgow University. He spent two years in Lancashire as a pupil of James Thomson who was one of the pioneers of the scientific industry. He developed an interest in the business of dyeing and calico printing and did more than anyone to elevate the trade into a science. His first paper 'Indigo,' published in 1823 in the "Annals of Philosophy," established his reputation and was translated into French and German. Crum established a department of Chemistry in Strathclyde University. He enjoyed the friendship of Thomas Thomson (see page 39) and Faraday and in 1844 he was elected a Fellow of the Royal Society of London. At the age of thirty in 1826 he married the youngest daughter of William Graham and they had four sons and one daughter: John Crum of Thornliebank, Walter Crum of Thornliebank, *Humphry Ewing Crum (Ewing), who succeeded his uncle James Ewing of Strathleven and took the name of Ewing, James Crum of Busby, and Margaret. During his life Crum never suffered from any illness but he died at Thornliebank aged 70 in 1867.

*Humphrey Ewing Crum Ewing died in 1882 and his monument is on the left in the lower photograph. On the right is the monument to his son Humphrey Ewing Crum Ewing jun who died in 1878 in a Sugar Plantation Estate in Demerara, Guyana, His body was sent home in a lead lined coffin filled with rum to preserve the body and is buried here.

COLIN DUNLOP 1775-1837
Design attributed to architect J T Rochhead
Upsilon Division

One of the early monuments in the Necropolis it was erected only a few
years after it opened and a family enclosure surrounds this stone.

Colin Dunlop was born in 1775 and became an advocate
but never practised as he purchased and successfully ran
Clyde Ironworks. He was a Whig politician, and one of the
great leaders of the Reform party in Glasgow. In 1835,
along with James Oswald, he was elected MP for the city.

He died, unmarried, in 1837 aged 62. On 'account of his
amiable qualities, his kindness to the poor and his liberal
political views' he was extremely popular and was honoured
with a public funeral and this monument to his memory.
He is commemorated in one of Alexander 'Sandie' Rodger's
(see page 131) poems poking fun at the 'cheerful blaze of
the Clyde Iron furnaces'
which lit up the skies
at night.

JAMES DUNLOP
Beta Division

Colin Dunlop's father
was James Dunlop
whose business was
mining, and, as a coal
master, worked the
minerals in Carmyle.
In 1810, he purchased
Tollcross House, and
died there in 1816.

JAMES BUCHANAN OF DOWANHILL
1755-1844
Designed by architect James Brown
(Brown and Carrick, architects)
Sculptor James Shanks
(also the sculptor for the Duncan Macfarlan Monument)
Upsilon Division

The upper part is based on the Choragic Monument of Lysicrates, one of many in the Necropolis. The Choragic Monument of Lysicrates near the Acropolis of Athens was erected by the Choragos Lysicrates, patron of many theatrical performances in the Theatre of Dionysus, to commemorate his award of first prize in 335 BC or 334 BC, to one of the performances he had sponsored. The Choragos was the sponsor who paid for and supervised the training of the dramatic dance-chorus.

In the hurricane on February 1856 this monument was the worst affected in the Necropolis. The whole of the upper structure was blown down and only the 'Tower of the Winds' was left. It was rebuilt with a solid circular body in the centre to ensure greater stability.

There are various members of the Buchanan family remembered here. James Buchanan of Dowanhill and John Buchanan, both of the 'eminent mercantile house of Buchanan and Dennistoun'. John was born in Drymen in Stirlingshire in 1755 and died at the age of 89 in 1844. His eldest son, George Buchanan (1802-1848) who owned the Stanley cotton mill near Perth which was established originally by David Dale is also buried here along with second son Thomas (1804-1864).

There is also another James Buchanan (1785-1857) who, after James Ewing, was the Merchants' House's next largest benefactor. The son of a Blacksmith he actually began working at the age of 15 for the above noted James Buchanan of Buchanan and Dennistoun. He was sent to the West Indies with a note to the manager there saying 'that he will either be the cleverest fellow or the greatest blackguard in the West Indies'. He eventually became the managing partner when the manager retired. He himself retired to Edinburgh, a very rich man at age of 31. He set up the Buchanan Institute in Glasgow for the education of destitute boys and in the 60 years of its existence educated 7,000 boys.

MAJOR ARCHIBALD DOUGLAS MONTEATH MAUSOLEUM d1842

HIS BROTHER JAMES MONTEATH DOUGLAS IS ALSO BURIED HERE

Designed by architect David Cousin

(Cousin & Gale, architects)

Upsilon Division

The 30ft diameter Mausoleum is based on the church of the holy Sepulchre in Cambridge. There are 48 Grotesque faces under the eaves and many more on the doorway. In Indian temple architecture the use of human faces is very common and they can be found on almost all Hindu temples but also on Palaces and Forts and are called Dwar-palas - Dwar means a door or direction, and Palas means guard. Every window design on the lower level is different but internally the monument is unfinished rubble work walls and the roof of the tower inside is brick. There are two covered vaults in the centre of the mausoleum where the two brothers lie side by side without any slab or inscription. There is not a single letter or date either on the inside or outside of this monument.

Major Archibald Douglas Monteath was an officer with the East India Company. There is a story that during one of the campaigns in India he captured an elephant loaded with treasure and that this money was used to buy two tenements on the corner of Buchanan Street and St Enoch's Square.

He retired to his native city, Glasgow, and when he retired he left between £800-£1000 for this monument to be built. His body lay in the Egyptian Vaults before this monument was completed.

Major Monteath's brother, James Monteath Douglas of Rosehall and Stonebyres who died in 1850, adopted the surname Douglas in order to inherit and continue the Douglas family name.

WILLIAM DUNN OF DUNTOCHER
1770-1849
Designed by architect J T Rochead
Sigma Division

This 40 ft high octagonal structure is formed from Irish granite in mural Roman style.

He was born in 1770 near Kirkintilloch in humble circumstances. Trained as a cotton spinner he was left an orphan at the age of 18 with four younger brothers and a younger sister to look after. From an early age he showed inventive skills and a good mind and he was employed in a machine shop. He then decided that if he sold the family home he could raise enough money to start his own business selling machinery to cotton spinning houses.

That proved very successful and in 1802 he bought a cotton spinning business in Calton, in 1808, he bought Duntocher Mill near Bowling and a few years later bought another in Faifley. In 1813, he bought an ironworks where he built Milton Mill and in 1831 he built Hardgate Mill nearby.

With the money he made he gradually bought various adjacent large estates which eventually extended two miles along the banks of the Clyde antagonising some of his neighbours in the process. He farmed 1200 acres of this land and employed 250 men.

He was said to be 'charitable without ostentation' and 'beloved as a gentleman of unassuming manners and kindly disposition'. He left a large sum to charities and the rest to his sole surviving brother Alexander who erected this monument to him.

REVEREND WILLIAM BRASH 1793-1851
Designed by architect John Bryce
Sigma Division

This is a tall, elaborate structure with the base supporting a short square pillar and an urn. Each of the 4 sides has a tablet of white marble with inscriptions. Above that is carved an open bible and several closed volumes piled on top of the pedestal.

William Brash was born in 1769, educated in Edinburgh and went to Edinburgh University. His first 'calling' was to the South of Scotland at the age of twenty one. He was 'called' to the church at East Campbell Street Glasgow, to assist the minister there who was quite frail and eventually took over the full ministry.

He was praised as an eloquent preacher and teacher of the young but developed a heart disease which made him unable to continue with his work and two years later he died quite suddenly of apoplexy in 1851 aged 58. The minister whom he had assisted outlived him and died at the age of 85 in 1852.

ANDREW BAIN, PRINTER

THOMAS BAIN, HIS BROTHER, 1816-1839
ROBERT BAIN, HIS BROTHER, 1822-1846
JANE FLEMING, HIS MOTHER, 1788-1854

ANDREW BAIN
1817 – 1858
JANE SYMINGTON, HIS WIFE
1817 – 1893
JAMES BAIN, THEIR SON
1841 – 1878

·NUNC LICET·

THE JAMES BELL STONE IS ON THE LEFT OF ANDREW BAIN'S AND IS BROKEN . IT IS SHOWN HERE IN THE INSERT AS IT MAY HAVE LOOKED

JAMES BELL 1806-1883
ANDREW BAIN 1817-1858
Omega Division

The monument to James Bell, an Iona cross is to the left of Bain's
Monument but is broken - a reconstruction is the insert.

The publishing company of Bell and Bain was established
in 1831 in Glasgow by partners James Bell and Andrew
Bain. Their original premises were in Bell Street, from
where they subsequently moved to Royal Exchange Square
and then to St Enoch Square. When St Enoch Station was
built, they found new premises in Mitchell Street.

Andrew Bain died at the age of 41 in 1858 and James Bell
remained sole partner until his death in 1883 after which
his son William Scott Bell took over the management until
his death in 1890. Bell and Bain then became a limited
company with the shares being given to the remaining
children. The Bell family are possibly related to the Bell
of Glasgow's Bell Pottery fame (see page 136).

Bell & Bain have made an important contribution to
printing in Glasgow, with many works on the city's history
bearing their name. A large number of books printed by
the company are preserved in the Andrew Bain Memorial
Collection which was presented to the Mitchell Library by
Andrew Bain's son. The business is still in existence today.

JAMES AND DAVID LAURIE
Designed by McLean of Clubb and McLean
Sigma Division

In 1802 brothers, James and David Laurie planned to
make their fortune by building a fashionable and exclusive
residential suburb with Carlton Place on the southern
riverfront as the showpiece.

The district on the south bank of the Clyde was named
after them and called Laurieston. Carlton Place contains
two elegant tenement buildings each of 375 feet in length,
with balconies in the middle and at the ends of their
facades and designed as a single architectural concept,
a first for Glasgow. The original architect was Peter
Nicholson, but it was completed by John Baird I.

Their uncle, John Laurie, lived in one of the centre houses,
No.52, called Laurieston House, which was deemed grand
enough to host George IV on his projected Glasgow trip of
1822. Unfortunately he never visited the city's finest interiors with Neo-classical plasterwork (now in a very danger-
ous state of repair) which had been created by the same
Italian artists who decorated Windsor Castle.

Much of the planned Laurieston was never completed but
some quality housing continued to be built after the
Laurie's plans were abandoned. In the 1830s houses in
Abbotsford Place had 7 or 8 rooms, with a mews for the
horse and carriage. But with the coming of the railways,
connected to new housing around the Queens Park area
to the south, further quality development ended.

DUGALD MOORE 1805-1841
Sculptor James Fillans
Omega Division

This literary Glasgow bookseller was born to humble
Highland parents in 1805. His father, a soldier, died
leaving Dugald's mother destitute. She did teach him
to read but he had to work from a very young age first
at a tobacco spinners and then as an apprentice in a
publishing company, James Lumsden & Son. James
Lumsden, who was made Lord Provost of Glasgow in
1843, noticed his poetic skills and Moore published
several books with help from his employer.

At the end of his apprenticeship he started his own
book selling business with help from friends and from
the money earned from his published work. Famous for
the poem 'The First Ship' which has been described as 'a
remarkable poem' by *Lyra Celtica and 'The Bard of the
North' from which came the lines for his epitaph. He
never married and he died suddenly aged 36.

His epitaph from a poem from his first book
'The Bard of the North'

'He was one
Schooled in adversity; he was reared
By her in winter and he went
Forth in the frosty pilgrimage of life,
To face its tempests, and to fling them back
With the strong arm of virtue and resolve.'

*Lyra Celtica was published by Patrick Geddes in 1896. The 'Celtic
Twilight' movement was dependent on ancient Gaelic tales and myths and
their revival and re-appropriation was a preoccupation for Geddes and the
artists and writers associated with him.

JOHN HENRY ALEXANDER
1796-1851
Designed by Alexander Kirkland/James Hamilton
Sculptor A. Handyside Ritchie (Fillans died before it was finished).
Omega Division

The monument is 24 ft high x 9 ft wide. This is an elaborate theatrical monument with a stage, complete with footlights and the figures of tragedy and comedy. Alexander, with laurel wreath, is featured above the stage and his friend, Mr James Hedderwick of the Glasgow Citizen, wrote the inscription.

Alexander was born in Perth in 1796 and was meant to follow his father's profession as a watch maker but when they moved to Glasgow he worked in his uncle's hosiery shop. His spare time was spent going to the theatre, performing and managing amateur productions. At the age of sixteen he made his first appearance in a professional theatre and three years later his performances in Edinburgh theatres, won him praise from Sir Walter Scott.

This actor/proprietor /manager eventually built and opened The Theatre Royal in Dunlop Street in 1840. He went on to perform and manage theatres all over Scotland and the North of England and he is also credited with perfecting The Great Gun Trick, the trick of catching a bullet in the teeth. In 1849 there was a false fire alarm. A door jammed and despite him being in the midst of the crowd roaring himself hoarse, 65 people died in the crush on a staircase and many more were injured. He never fully recovered.

He handed the management over and died in 1851 aged 55. The Theatre Royal did burn down in 1863 but was immediately rebuilt. It was finally taken down in 1869 by a railway company.

THOMAS ATKINSON 1801-1833
Omega Division

A pyramid terminating in a flame and bearing on the white marble panel a ship and a dove bearing an olive branch in its mouth and the inscription, 'As forth the dove went trembling'

To the memory of
THOMAS ATKINSON BOOKSELLER
Who died
At sea while on a voyage to Barbados
for the recovery of his health
10th October 1833
in the 32nd year of his age

While when beneath the verge of time
I've sped - as soon I know 'twill be - I rise but in another clime
Uncircilin - fixed eternity

This simple tribute
To the genuine worth of an only son
Is placed here
By his early widowed now bereaved
and desolate mother AMA

This poet and writer was born of humble parents in Glasgow in 1801. He worked himself up from apprentice bookseller to owner of a bookselling business. He was also a recognised author and a great speaker. He developed consumption at an early age and he sold up and sailed for Barbados. He died during the journey and was buried at sea in the oak coffin he had taken with him.

He left a legacy both to his mother and to trustees to set up an Atkinsonian Institute for education in languages and literature for artisans but unfortunately it never became a physical reality and the money was used to set up bursaries for the Royal College of Science and Technology.

Despite dying at the age of thirty two he has his books as his lasting legacy, 'The Sextuple Alliance' and 'The Chameleon' being the best known.

REVEREND DR JOHN DICK 1764-1833
Designed by architect Robert Black
Sculptor David Buchanan
Omega Division

Another Monument based on the Choragic Monument of Lysicrates, Athens.
A central urn and finial are missing. The monument was erected five years
after his death.

TRANSLATION OF THE GREEK INSCRIPTION ON THE FRIEZE :
O tell me not the good man dies
Embalmed in sacred sleep he lies

The Reverend Dr John Dick was born in Aberdeen in 1764
where his father was also a minister. He was the eldest of
nine children and at the age of twenty one he was licensed
as a preacher by the Presbytery of Perth and Dunfermline.

He was ordained at the age of twenty three in Slateford
near Edinburgh where he preached for fifteen years.
He married Jane Coventry and they had six sons and four
daughters.

He was 'called' to take over the ministry in Aberdeen on
his father's death but instead was sent by the Synod to
become minister of the Secession church of Greyfriars, one
of the most important churches in Glasgow, where he
preached for over 30 years. He produced four volumes of
Lectures in Theology which were well received and were
published by his son after his death. He died, aged 69, of
inflammation of the brain caused by an inner ear infection
and is buried in Glasgow Cathedral graveyard.

The architect Robert Black's own
monument is near here.

REVEREND DUNCAN MACFARLAN
1771-1857
Designed by architect Jonathan Anderson Bell
Bronze portrait panel by William Brodie
Sculptor James Shanks
Kappa Division

This tower raised by public subscription commemorates the
Reverend Duncan Macfarlan. Macfarlan was born in 1771
in Drymen where his father was minister. From the age of
twelve he studied at Glasgow University and obtained an
MA in 1788. In 1797, at the age of twenty five, he married
his cousin Ann Allan who was four years younger than him
and they had a family of five boys and four girls. She died at
the age of thirty six. Macfarlan graduated in divinity at the
University of Glasgow and in 1806 and 1810 he was
appointed Dean of Faculties.

In 1815 he became one of the King's Chaplains for
Scotland, and four years later was elected Moderator of the
General Assembly. When he became Principal and Vice
Chancellor of Glasgow University in 1823 he resigned his
charge at Drymen but he was then appointed minister of
Glasgow Cathedral and he held both positions for the next
thirty four years. He was a popular man in Glasgow and a
testimonial dinner with 400 guests was held in his honour
in 1842. He wrote an inscription to celebrate the laying of
the foundation stone of the Bridge of Sighs and he wel-
comed Queen Victoria to Glasgow Cathedral in 1849. An
event recorded on the base of her statue in George Square.

He retired in 1840, but was persuaded to return on being
elected Moderator for a second time in 1842. He died in

JOHN LEADBETTER 1788-1865
Kappa Division

John Leadbetter's father was a wright by trade in Penicuik and shortly after he was born in 1788 his parents moved to Lanark. He wanted to study in Glasgow but transport from Lanark was twice a week by covered carrier's cart, which didn't have springs, so whenever he visited his family he walked the twenty-four miles.

Leadbetter became a clerk in a linen trade business, studied French in the evenings eventually becoming a partner in the company. He was now well established in the linen trade and formed his own company in 1815. With the coming of power-looms the business expanded and John Leadbetter & Co. eventually opened branches in Dundee and Belfast.

From 1832-1846 he was on the Glasgow Town Council, and was Lord Dean of Guild in 1844 and 1845.

He was an enthusiastic supporter of railways and wanted to see them established in Scotland, becoming Chairman of the Directors of the Edinburgh and Glasgow Railway, which was formally opened in 1842. He retired from the Chairmanship shortly afterwards, disapproving of trains being run on Sundays. He was also a Director of the Ayrshire Railway Company and Chairman of the Dumfries Railway.

In 1848 he became ill and he died in Torquay several years

JOHN KNOX MONUMENT ERECTED 1825
Designer W Warren
Architect Thomas Hamilton
Sculptor Robert Forrest
Kappa Division

A 12 ft high statue of John Knox, in Geneva gown, holding a bible in his left hand on a 58ft high Doric column. This monument was erected in Fir Park before the cemetery opened. The ceremony for the foundation stone being laid was witnessed by 10,000 people in the Cathedral graveyard.

John Knox was born in 1515 near Edinburgh and educated at St Andrew's University. In 1543 he was an ordained Catholic priest but in 1545 he publicly professed the Protestant faith. In 1546 Knox was a Scottish Protestant refugee, taken prisoner and for 18 months forced to row French galleys permanently injuring his health. After a time of voluntary exile in England he married Marjorie Bowes in 1555 and travelled to Geneva. The Roman Catholic Church was overthrown by the Scottish parliament of 1560 and Protestantism was established.

Knox formulated the Confession of Faith and drew up the Constitution. Knox's view that it was quite legitimate to overthrow and execute female rulers did not endear him to Mary Queen of Scots and she had Knox arrested and put on trial for conspiracy but he was acquitted. His wife died in 1559 and in 1564 Knox, aged fifty one, married seventeen year old Margaret Stewart and lived a very well paid busy life. A testimony to Knox at St. Giles was given by the Earl of Mortoun, the Regent of Scotland :

"Here lyeth a man who in his life never feared the face of man, who hath been often threatened with dagge and dagger, but yet hath ended his dayes in peace and honour."

The site of John Knox's grave at St Giles has been covered over by a car park for the adjacent Parliament Hall. He is buried under parking bay number 23.

JAMES EWING OF STRATHLEVEN
1775-1853
Designed by architect John Baird
Sculptor J Mossman
Kappa Division

The monument as we see it today seems very plain but its proximity to John
Knox signifies its importance. It consists of a sarcophagus of polished
Peterhead granite originally covered in beautiful bronze ornamentation and
bronze bas-relief panels which are now missing but were described as follows:

Facing north towards John Knox is the inscription to James Ewing.

Facing south was a medallion portrait flanked by symbolic figures of
Commerce and Art/Literature

Facing east and west were representations of Education and Charity.

James Ewing was born in 1774 and was a very important
man to Glasgow. He was Lord Dean of Guild on two occa-
sions - 1815 and 1830 - which in itself was very unusual.
He was Lord Provost of the city in 1831 and one of the
first two elected representatives, following the Reform Act,
in the House of Commons for Glasgow between
1832-1835.

In his mansion, which is now the site of Queen Street
station, he discussed John Strang's idea for the Necropolis
with Mr Dennistoun of Golfhill, Mr MacKenzie of Craigpark,
Laurence Hill, the collector of the Merchants' House and
Mr Douglas of Barloch all of whom have monuments or are
buried in the Necropolis. In 1836 he retired at the age of
60, married a Miss Crawford and bought an estate called
Levenside, which he renamed Strathleven, near
Dumbarton. He died aged 78 leaving a fortune of
£280,000, much of it to charities.

DENNISTOUN FAMILY
Omega division

The Dennistoun monument was described in 1857 as follows: 'grassy plot surrounded by a chain supported on eight blocks of Argyllshire granite.' The monument is no longer here but its proximity to John Knox just to the east (back to back with Rev Thomas Brown's sarcophagus) is again important. Mr Dennistoun was one of the people at James Ewings mansion that day to discuss developing Fir Park into the Necropolis.

At the beginning of the 19th century, James Dennistoun (1759-1835) of Colgrain moved to Glasgow from the district of Campsie to make his fortune.

As well as running his mercantile business in 1809 he set up the Glasgow Bank which he managed. This was later merged into the Union Bank of Scotland.

James Dennistoun retired in 1829 and the merchants of Glasgow gave him a magnificent dinner in the Royal Exchange and 'requested to be allowed the honor of having his portrait painted and engraved for distribution among them.' He died in 1835 at Golfhill House.

His eldest son Alexander Dennistoun (1790-1874) lived in Golfhill House, which was just to the east of the Necropolis, after his father's death. He also inherited the family business in Glasgow and in 1828 opened offices in both New York and Paris. Both Alexander and his brother John became MPs for the city. He was also responsible for buying various neighbouring estates to Golfhill and building the area called Dennistoun in Glasgow. On the death of his younger sister Mary he inherited an estate near Gareloch where he spent a lot of time painting with his brothers James and John. He died aged 84 in 1874.

DENNISTOUN

This area of Glasgow, a mile east from the city centre, was built by Alexander Dennistoun in the 1860's on several estate lands he had acquired at different times. The first purchase was Golfhill by James Dennistoun, Alexander's father, who bought it from the trustees of Jonathan Anderson in 1814 and built the mansion called Golfhill House, just to the east of the Necropolis, where he lived till his death in 1835. Alexander purchased the adjoining lands of Annfield, Whitehill, Broompark, Reidvale and Craigpark until the total estate extended to over 200 acres. In 1861 Dennistoun employed the architect, James Salmon, to design and set out the plan for the Dennistoun area of Glasgow and he designed an elegant suburb of the city with handsome entrance gates, villas, gardens and terraces.

The development began with Annfield Place and was quickly followed by the first villa, Fern Villa, on Westercraigs. Further villas, terraces and gardens were built on and between Westercraigs and Craigpark which now forms the Conservation Area of Dennistoun. Tenements were ultimately built on the rest of the land east of Whitehill Street and many of the streets of Dennistoun are named after members of the Dennistoun family.

REVEREND DR THOMAS BROWN
1776-1847
Designed by architect J T Rochead
Omega Division

The stone is from Craigend Quarry and is in the form of a 7' x 3'
sarcophagus on a series of steps. The only ornament is Graecian fret in
banded work.

Thomas Brown was born in Closeburn, near Dumfries and
studied in Edinburgh before moving to Kirkcudbright and
marrying Miss Eliza Duncan in 1808. They had two
children but one died in infancy.

For nearly 20 years he preached there before being offered
and taking on the role at St John's church in Glasgow in
1826. He was known as "the meek Christian philosopher."

His 'spirituality, wisdom, and shrewdness' endeared him to
all. When Dr. Brown seceded from the established Church
more than three-quarters of his people followed him joining
the Free Church of Scotland and they built a church for
him on a site on the south side of George Street, Glasgow.

Dr. Brown was elected as the second moderator of the Free
Church of Scotland. He died in 1847.

REVEREND WILLIAM BLACK 1801-1851
Designed by J T Emmett of London
Omega Division

On white stone on a high pedestal supported by 4 columns of Derbyshire marble lies a statue of the deceased. This was one of the most striking monuments in the Necropolis but is now missing the spectacular 30ft canopy - see the small image above.

The following is a description of the monument as it was in 1857 :
"The whole is covered by a bold eaves roof protected by zinc and surmounted by 2 gilt crosses" " the interior of the canopy is painted a rich azure". "There are no pinnacles or other extraneous feature and carved enrichments are limited to the bold but varied capitals of the columns, a delicate band of foliage round the arches, some quaint bosses in the groining and a rich leaf moulding round the tomb. The names of the apostles and the cardinal virtues are sculpted in scrolls around the capitals and there are angels at each corner. The canopy was removed for structural reasons.

The base reliefs
North - the entombment of Christ
South - the resurrection of Christ
West - Mary in the garden receiving Christ's message
East - Apostles

William Black was born in 1801 in Auchinairn, near Glasgow. He entered Glasgow University at the age of eleven and completed his studies at the age of fifteen. He preached first at a Church in Hamilton, then Shettleston and eventually became sole minister of the *Barony Church in 1838.

He married a daughter of William Young, and died of consumption while travelling for the sake of his health in Florence aged 50. He had requested a small funeral but a large number of people turned up to pay their respects.

*The congregation originally worshiped in the crypt of the Cathedral but eventually built a Church which was near the present position of the Necropolis Gates. They then used the Crypt as a burial ground for a time.

REVEREND ROBERT MUTER 1771-1842
Designed by architect John Stephen
(Scott, Stephen & Gale, architects)
Omega Division

The symbolism of winged hourglass and inverted torches is shown
clearly here above the columns.

The Reverend Dr Robert Muter was born in 1771
and was 'called' by the Duke Street United Associate
Congregation in 1800. He was one of the most popular
preachers of his day and they had to build a bigger
place of worship to accommodate the congregation.
In the twenty years that he preached there the place was
filled to overflowing.

He picked the site for his monument from where he
could view his residence in Broompark, now part of
the conservation area of Dennistoun, where his
family continued to live after his death. He died
aged 71 in 1842.

AGNES GILMOUR 1816-1849
ALLAN GILMOUR 1805-1884
Sculptor G Mossman
Omega Division

A sandstone obelisk, erected in 1851, with a carving of four children, gazing at a memorial inscribed 'Beloved Mother' on the south-face. The oldest, the girl in the middle, is holding a baby on her knee and the other two, are boys dressed in petticoats, which was the fashion at that time and have slightly shorter hair than their sister. There is no other inscription on the monument.

Agnes Strang, the wife of Allan Gilmour, died in childbirth aged thirty three. She left behind three young children and a baby.

Allan Gilmour was forty four when his wife died in 1849 and the children continued to live with him in their house in St Vincent Street. He was a wealthy ship owner and merchant.

One branch of the Gilmour family had established a successsful business in New Brunswick, Canada, acquiring extensive stretches of forest where timber was easily available. They also opened up a chain of sawmills which processed the trees for use in ship-building.

At the age of sixteen, he was sent on one of his family's ships to join the expanding business in Canada and was promoted, eventually becoming a partner. He wrote a book, describing a tour of America he undertook when he was twenty four, called 'Remarks and Observations by Allan Gilmour on a Tour of America in 1829'. When he eventually retired he moved to Park Gardens in the West End of Glasgow where he died in 1884 aged 79. He had never remarried and he was buried here alongside his wife.

The obelisk on the right to Dr William Couper, a surgeon and partner in St Rollox Works, whose 3 sons married Tennants daughters.

CHARLES TENNANT 1768-1838
Sculptor Patric Park
Omega Division

Many amusing comments are made about this monument - at the time it was described as 'an attitude expressive of meditation'

Charles Tennant of *St. Rollox, was one of the founders of the great chemical trade of Glasgow. Born in 1768 in Ayrshire and family friends of Robert Burns, he trained as a silk weaver but moved to Darnley where he established his own bleaching fields. In 1795 Tennant married Margaret Wilson who lived near his bleaching fields, and they had a family of ten children.

In 1798 he tried to take out a patent for a liquid bleach but it was refused. However, in 1799, with the help of chemist Charles MacIntosh (1766–1843), who invented the water-proof material that bears his name, Tennant patented a bleach powder and in 1800 he established a chemical works at St Rollox which became the largest chemical works in the world. By 1815 it was known as Charles Tennant and Co and expanded into other chemicals, metallugy and explosives. He took an intense pride and interest in the business and he died in 1838 aged 70. The chemical business became known as the United Alkali Company Ltd. and eventually merged with others in 1926 to form the chemical giant Imperial Chemical Industries (ICI).

*St. Roque or Roch (St Rollox) was born at the end of the 13c. He had the ability to cure the plague and is honoured in France and Italy. There was a church dedicated to St. Roch on the site of the St Rollox Works.

CHARLES STREET Named after Charles Tennant
TENNANT STREET Named after Charles Tennant

CHARLES MACINTOSH 1766-1843

Charles Macintosh was born in 1766. His father George came from the Highlands, moving to Glasgow to set up a factory in Dennistoun in 1777 to manufacture a red dying powder made from lichens called Cudbear. Charles had a strong interest in chemistry and In 1818, while analysing the by-products of a works making coal gas, he discovered dissolved india rubber. He joined two sheets of fabric together with this solution, allowed them to dry, and discovered that the new material was waterproof. Chemist George Hancock and Macintosh solved many of the problems involved in reliably producing waterproofed sheets and coats. The material was introduced in 1824 and Macintosh founded his own waterproofing company in Glasgow in 1834 but moved to Manchester in 1840.

Although Macintosh is best known for his waterproof material, he was a brilliant chemist. He invented a bleaching powder along with Charles Tennant of the St Rollox Chemical Works, devised a way of using carbon gases to convert malleable iron to steel and worked out a hot-blast process with James Neilson to produce high quality cast iron.

His father, George, mother, Mary and grandfather, Provost John Anderson and other members of the family are all buried in the Cathedral graveyard.

DUNCHATTAN STREET - This is formed on the lands of Dunchattan, just to the west of Dennistoun, of which George Macintosh was the owner. The name means the hill of the Cattanach or Clan Chattan, of which Macintosh was chief.

FRENCH STREET - It was at first called Papillon Street, after Pierre Jacques Papillon, who was brought from Rouen in France in 1785 by George Macintosh to explain the secret of Turkey-red dye.

MACINTOSH STREET - It was formed on the lands of Dunchattan.

WILLIAM RAE WILSON 1772-1849
Designed by architect Jonathan Anderson Bell
Alpha Division

This 27 ft high, octagonal, domed Moorish kiosk is similar to
sepulchral monuments in Palestine. It is constructed from liver-rock
from the Binnie quarry. No wood, iron or lead was used in the
concealed joints. Inside are inscriptions and the family arms of
Rae and Wilson.

William Rae (or Ray) was born in Paisley in 1772
but was decended from a family from Haddington.
He practiced as a solicitor and took the name Wilson when
he inherited from his uncle John Wilson (one of the Town
Clerks of Glasgow) in 1806.

After the death of his wife, Frances Phillips, who died
eighteen months after their marriage, he went travelling to
recover from his grief and he wrote the very successful book
'Travels in the Holy Land' to much acclaim. He also wrote
many other travel books. He did marry again and his second
wife, Miss Cates, accompanied him on his travels.

He had an honorary doctorate conferred on him some years
before he died and he left a sum of money for an annual
prize to a student of the best religious essay. He died in
London in 1849 but his wife had this monument built and
he is buried here.

His Will instructed that the rest of his family be removed
from the Ramshorn churchyard to be interred here after
rumours that the railway line was going to be driven
through that graveyard.

JOHN HOULDSWORTH OF CRANSTONHILL
1807-1859 - FAMILY MAUSOLEUM
Designed by architect/sculptor John Thomas
Alpha Division

On the right Charity carrying a child and on the left Hope with an anchor.
Inside are three marble figures - Faith in the centre with an angel on each side.

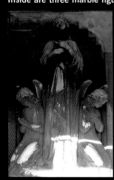

Henry Houldsworth came to Glasgow from Nottingham in 1799 to manage a cotton mill in North Woodside and became the owner in 1801. By 1805 he had constructed the largest steam powered mill in Glasgow in the Bridgeton area. 30 years on and the textile industry was diminishing so he set up a mechanics shop in John Street. This developed into the iron works known as the Anderston Foundry which was in business until 1930. He married Jane Richardson and they had two sons before coming to Glasgow. Their third son John, was born in Glasgow in the Cranstonhill Mansion in Anderson. Both Henry and John were Provosts of Anderson before the district was annexed by Glasgow.

John, the man remembered here was born in 1807, and educated in Glasgow, Geneva and Heidelberg. In 1836 he married Eliza Muir and they had three sons and two daughters. When the district of Anderson was annexed and became part of Glasgow he became a Senior Baillie of Glasgow.

Two years before he died he bought No.1 Park Terrace and planned to have it furnished elaborately. The magnificence was discussed so much that Queen Victoria and Prince Albert visited the designer's studios. When she left Victoria said, "You say the gentleman's name is Houldsworth. It ought to be Goldsworth." Unfortunately he died in 1859, aged 52, before it was finished. He was a keen yachtsman, a musician and supporter of many artists. He was remembered to be 'never seen out of temper' and was liked 'for his uprightness and fairness' in business.

HOULDSWORTH STREET - It is named after Henry Houldsworth

69

REV GEORGE MARSHALL MIDDLETON
1826-1866
Designed by architect Alexander 'Greek' Thomson
Sculptor J Mossman
Alpha Division

The congregation subscribed £75 for both this and the monument to the
Reverend AO Beattie (see page 24) in the Necropolis to be designed by
Alexander 'Greek' Thomson.

Born in Glasgow in 1826. At the age of 24 he was 'called'
to the United Presbyterian church at Kinross. He was there
for five years and then appointed colleague and successor
to the Rev Beattie in 1855 in a co-pastorate role. When
Beattie died in 1858 he became one of the 'brightest young
ministers' and the first to preach at 'Greek' Thomson's St
Vincent St Church when it opened in 1859. However his
health failed and he died at the age of 40 in 1866.

WALTER MACFARLANE 1817-1885
Sculptor Bertram MacKennal
Zeta Division

Walter Macfarlane I was buried in the Necropolis in 1885, although his monument, which features a bronze portrait panel was not erected until 1896. The panel under the portrait features symbolism about death and resurrection. The woman pouring the water away indicates life fading away and the sun rising indicates resurrection. The two winged heads symbolise the departure of the soul.

Walter Macfarlane I was born in Torrance of Campsie, near Glasgow, and started work with a jeweller, William Russell, before serving an apprenticeship with the blacksmith, James Buchanan. He then spent some 10 years working for Moses, McCulloch & Co's Cumberland Foundry before setting up his own Saracen Foundry (see page 151) with partners Thomas Russell and James Marshall.

Macfarlane was also involved in politics becoming the President of the Glasgow Liberal Association and a Glasgow Councillor. His former home in Park Circus is now the Registry office for the City of Glasgow. In 1880, Macfarlane's nephew, Walter Macfarlane II (1853-1932), who joined the firm in 1871, became a partner and adopted son and later succeeded to the firm on the death of his uncle in 1885.

CHARLES CLARK MACKIRDY 1811-1891
Designed by architect James Thomson
(Baird and Thomson architects)
Sculptor David Buchanan
Zeta Division

This is another monument based on The Choragic Monument of Lysicrates. It has a Corinthian rotunda with fine granite detail. The door is cast iron set in smooth rusticated masonry.

Charles Clark MacKirdy's parents were John MacKirdy and Mary Eliott who married in 1801 and lived at Birkwood, a castellated mansion, situated on the river Nethan in Lanarkshire. John was a successful merchant with considerable estates in *British Guiana.

Charles was the second son who owned a successful cotton spinning company and lived in Blythswood Square, Glasgow, till his death at the age of 80 in 1891. He had succeeded to the estate of Birkwood on the death of his eldest brother, John, in 1881, but he found that it 'did not suit his health to reside there' and made over the property to his younger brother, General David Elliott MacKirdy.

David Elliott MacKirdy, was a General in the Army, and Colonel of the 69th Regiment. He served in the East and West Indies and Canada in Command of that Regiment, taking it from the West Indies to India, in 1857, and to Canada in 1867. His monument was also designed by James Thomson and is in Lesmahagow Cemetery.

*British Guiana was the name of the British colony on the northern coast of South America, now the independent nation of Guyana.

"MacKirdy, or Mackirdy, formerly MaKurerdy or Makwrerdy was an ancient Scottish surname in the island of Bute.

ALEXANDER ALLAN 1825-1890
MONUMENT BUILT 1894-9
Sculptor James Pittendrigh Macgillivray
Masons Alexander MacDonald and Co
Zeta Division

These bronze angels are my favourite pieces of sculpture in the Necropolis.
Unfortunately the bronze portrait panel, also by J Pittendrigh Macgillivray,
of Alexander and Jane Allan is missing.

The founder of the shipping company, The Allan Line,
which ran Transatlantic Liners, was Alexander (Sandy) Allan
who was born in Fairlie. He was apprenticed to a shoemaker
before moving to Saltcoats as a ship's carpenter which he
gave up to go to sea. Within a few years he became Master
and part owner of several small ships. His first transatlantic
trip was in 1819 and under his direction and that of his
sons, the Allan Line progressed from wooden sailing ships
to iron-built steamships and from a one-man operator to
a leading transatlantic company. Sandy Allan died in 1854,
aged 74.

His sons, James, Hugh, Andrew, Bryce and Alexander, named
in order from oldest to youngest, took over the business and
the Glasgow office was run by James and Alexander. James
retired and under the direction of Alexander, whose
monument this is, the business continued to expand
throughout the second half of the 19th century until by 1884

DAVID EDMUND OUTRAM 1818-1893
Zeta Division

This monument is to David Edmund Outram, born in 1818 and founder of a firm of stockbrokers. His son was Lieutenant-Colonel James Outram, Honorary Colonel of the late 1st V.B.H.L.I. and his uncle was George Outram, editor of *The Glasgow Herald until 1856.

George Outram (1805 - 1856), was a humorous poet, and a Scottish advocate as well as the editor of *The Glasgow Herald.

He privately printed in 1851 'Lyrics, Legal and Miscellaneous', which were published with a memoir in 1874. Many of his pieces are highly amusing, the poem 'The Annuity' being one of the best.

*The Glasgow Herald is one of the oldest newspapers in Glasgow, beginning its life as the `Glasgow Advertiser' in January 1783, changing briefly to the title `Herald and Advertiser and Commercial Chronicle' in 1803 before becoming the `Glasgow Herald' on 26th August 1804. It is the longest continuously published daily newspaper in Britain

MALCOLM CAMPBELL 1848-1935
Zeta Division

Fruit is interlaced here in the design of this Iona Cross

Malcolm Campbell was born in 1848. He began working for the greengrocer Mark Walker in his fruit shop in Gordon Street in Glasgow in 1864 and when Walker retired in 1878 he bought the shop from him. He sold tomatoes, grown at the firm's own nurseries, but also imported a great variety and quantity of fruit from the Continent.

These imports of perishable goods required a new sort of distribution system and Malcolm Campbell, sold cheap groceries and fruit such as melons, grapes and bananas to the working class and introduced the first example of the modern "multiple" shop chains combining the wholesale and retail. He eventually had a chain of grocery, fruit and vegetable shops across Scotland.

The main shop in Gordon Street, near Central Station, had fantastic window displays and one of the promotions included a banana tree in the 1880s. The company became known as Malcolm Campbell Ltd in 1899. He became Sir Malcolm Campbell in 1922 and died in 1935 aged 87.

JAMES MERRY Jnr 1805-1877
Zeta Division

James Merry Jnr. was born in 1805, educated at Glasgow University and married Anne, eldest daughter of James McHardy of Glenboig. He was a coal master and in 1836, when he became sole proprietor of the family's Glasgow-based coal business, he formed a partnership that became Merry & Cunningham. By the end of the decade the firm was the second largest coal company and the third largest iron company in Scotland.

In 1857 he failed to win a Parliamentary seat in Glasgow. but became Liberal MP for the Falkirk Burghs in the second General Election that year, only to be stripped of the seat after an inquiry into corrupt practices. He was re-elected in 1859 and served in Parliament until 1874.

He was a great gambling man and he started with fighting cocks which he bred himself before going onto his great love which was horses. He owned two Derby winners and in 1873 his horses won the Derby, Oaks and St Leger winning a huge sum of money. Most of his money was invested in landed estates and in 1857 he made his home at Belladrum near Beauly, Invernesshire. In 1858 he had extensive sym-metrical additions made to the house by architect David Bryce and he also had extensive work done to the gardens. James Merry Jnr was an MP, Deputy Lieutenant and Justice of the Peace. He died in 1877 aged 72.

The house is now demolished but Mrs Merry, 1824-1911, had a small chapel built on the estate in the shape of a temple designed by architect RFJ Fairlie in 1935 which still remains.

On the gravestones:

JOHN BURNS MACBRAYNE OF GLENBRANTER
DIED 18TH NOVEMBER 1900, AGED 67.
MAGDALENE LIDDELL, HIS WIFE
DIED 26TH JANUARY 1892, AGED 71.
WILLIAM LIDDELL MACBRAYNE, THEIR SON
DIED 3RD MARCH 1861, AGED 22
ELIZABETH LIDDELL MACBRAYNE, THEIR DAUGHTER
DIED 11TH MARCH 1926, AGED 72.
ALSO
ISABELLA LIDDELL,
DIED 7TH FEBRUARY 1892, AGED 74.
ELIZABETH MARGARET HENDERSON,
DIED 4TH JUNE 1893, AGED 63.
ALSO IN MEMORY OF
DAVID MACBRAYNE, ELDEST SON
THE ABOVE JOHN BURNS MACBRAYNE
DIED 8TH JUNE 1907, AGED 56
BURIED IN RHU PARISH CHURCHYARD.

DAVID MACBRAYNE
SHIPOWNER, GLASGOW
BORN 28TH NOV. 1817, DIED 26TH JAN. 1907,
AND OF HIS WIFE
ROBINA ECKFORD ROBERTSON
DIED 4TH OCT. 1878, AGED 39 YEARS
WHO LIE HERE.
ALSO OF
DAVID HOPE MACBRAYNE
BORN 5TH MARCH 1862, DIED 1ST APRIL 193?
BURIED IN THE DEAN CEMETERY, EDINBUR

DAVID MACBRAYNE 1817-1907
Epsilon Division

David MacBrayne' father Donald was from the Highlands and became a partner in a calico and linen printers in Currie's Closs, High Street, which afterwards became MacBrayne, Stenhouse & Cowas. David married the daughter of John Burns, of the Barony Church and was the nephew of George Burns who sold him the only asset that he ever sold, the Western Isles Line, now known as Caledonian MacBrayne.

George Burns, (1795 – 1891) was an ambitious evangelical Christian and his story is much more interesting. He was born in Glasgow and formed a business partnership with his brother James Burns (1789 - 1871). They started sailing ships between Glasgow and Liverpool and across the Atlantic to Canada and the USA. J. & G. Burns also set up the regular steamer service to the Inner and Outer Hebrides which was sold to David MacBrayne in mid-1870s.

J. & G. Burns were general merchants in the 1820s and ran the mails between Greenock, Liverpool, Belfast and Londonderry making a lot of money. In the 1830s, Samuel Cunard, a Boston merchant seeking funding for a mail shipping line between Liverpool and the U.S., visited George Burns having been rejected by both Wall Street and the City of London. Burns founded a consortium investing £270,000 – (£10,500 of his own money) and by 1839 was the first Chairman of the Cunard Steam Packet Company. It had guaranteed Government contracts and the Cunard Line expanded rapidly. Burns decided to buy out the consortium and at that time he also acquired the Castle Wemyss estate at Wemyss Bay a few miles north of Largs. By late 1854 the mail business, which was funding the buy-out of the Cunard consortium, was threatened by the rival Ardrossan Line which, with the Glasgow & S Western Railway Company, proposed a Parliamentary Bill to incorporate timetabling of rail and boats for faster delivery of passengers and mails to and from Ireland. George Burns decided to fight that Bill. He wrote to Viscount Canning, Postmaster General in April 1855, and suggested the Bill be thrown out "I dread opposition from incorporated rail roads and steamboats." He testified shortly after this to a Parliamentary Committee. It is thought that Anthony Trollope stayed at Castle Wemyss that winter to advise on fighting the Bill. The amendment was thrown out by the Committee and Burns later took over the Ardrossan Line.

John Burns, George and James' older brother, was among fifty people who died when the steamship Orion sank off Portpatrick in June 1850, on its way from Liverpool to Glasgow. (see page 85)

HENRY DUBS d1876
Zeta Division

Dübs & Co. was a locomotive works in Glasgow, founded by Henry Dübs, a German engineer, in 1863. He died in 1876. The company evolved into the Queen's Park Locomotive Works and in 1903 became part of the North British Locomotive Company, based first in Hydepark Street in Anderson, and then in Springburn employing over 7,000 people.

Locomotives built by Dübs are still in existence today and eleven of them are locomotives which were built for the New Zealand Railways Department. Numerous others can be found in South Africa and the Isle of Man.

WILLIAM JAMES CHRYSTAL 1854-1921
Zeta Division

I've included this for the incredible Angel. Angels are normally portrayed as male but this one is an exception.

William Chrystal's father, Robert Chrystal was the son-in-law of John White, the founder of the Shawfield Chemical Works.

William was born in Glasgow in 1854, and educated at Glasgow Academy and Glasgow University and in 1873 undertook training in a chemical laboratory. He then joined his grandfather's Shawfield Works as a trained and expert chemist, and a few years later, on the death of his uncle, also John White, he became technical partner of the company.

He married Marion Lennox, daughter of John Alexander of Glasgow, and they had two sons and two daughters.

Chrystal invented many improvements in manufacturing and took out many patents, one in particular of crystallized bichromate of soda. It was through his efforts and inventions that Shawfield Works expanded to be the largest of their kind in the world. He was a member of Glasgow Chamber of Commerce and Chairman of the Royal Exchange. He bought the estate of Auchendennan on Loch Lomondside and refurbished the mansion in which he died, in 1921, aged 67.

JOHN ELDER MONUMENT 1824-1869
Designed by John Honeyman
Sculptor Anderson and Co
Epsilon Division

John Elder was born in Glasgow 1824, the son of a mechanical engineer who had built a succession of engines for ocean-going ships.

After serving his apprenticeship, Elder worked for a time as a draughtsman in England. He returned to Glasgow in 1848 and ran his father's drawing office before, in 1852, joining Randolph Elliott & Co as a partner. This firm of millwrights, later renamed John Elder & Co, moved into shipbuilding and 111 sets of steam engines were built at the Fairfield Yard during Elder's time. Elder was a leader in marine architecture and steamship construction, and headed an engineering operation which employed several thousand skilled workmen.

Elder was known for good worker relations and for providing education and an accident fund. After his death in 1869 aged 45 his wife Isabella (Ure) Elder, herself a lawyer, added to the endowment of the Chair of Civil Engineering and Applied Mechanics in the University of Glasgow and also provided an endowment for the new Chair of Naval Architecture. She donated Elder Park and Elder Library to the area of Govan (opened by Andrew Carnegie) and the park contains statues of both of them

JAMES SHERIDAN KNOWLES 1784 -1862
Zeta Division

This actor appeared in Mr Alexander's Theatre in Dunlop Street and the monument at each corner has sculptured heads of some of his most famous characters eg William Tell and Emma.

He was born in Cork in 1784 and his family moved to London in 1793. At the age of fourteen Knowles published a popular ballad entitled "The Welsh Harper".

He obtained a medical degree and although offered a share in a practice, he left medicine for the stage, making his first appearance in Bath, and played Hamlet at the Crow Theatre, Dublin. In 1809, in Wexford, he married Maria Charteris, an actress from the Edinburgh Theatre. Edmund Kean appeared in his play 'Leo' which he wrote in 1810 and another play, 'Brian Boroihme', written for the Belfast Theatre in the next year, drew good crowds, but his earnings were so small that he became assistant to his father at the Belfast Academical Institution.

In 1817 he moved from Belfast to Glasgow, where, besides running a school, he continued to write for the stage. His first real success was 'Caius Gracchus', in Belfast in 1815. 'Virginius' was written for Edmund Kean and was first performed in 1820 at Covent Garden.

His best-known play, 'The Hunchback', was produced at Covent Garden in 1832. Eventually he left the stage and became a Baptist preacher who attracted large audiences and for some years received an annual pension of £200, given by Sir Robert Peel. He died at Torquay in 1862. His works were privately printed by his son, Richard Brinsley Knowles (1820-1882), who was a well known journalist

ROBERT BAIRD OF AUCHMEDDON
1806-1856
Epsilon Division

There are a number of monuments in the Necropolis which are based on the design of the tomb of Scipio Barbatus in Rome and are in the form of an altar. The one at the top here is for Robert Baird.

Robert Baird's father Alexander, was a tenant farmer in Monkland. He married Jean Moffat and had a family of two daughters, Janet Baird and Jane Baird, and eight sons - in order of seniority - William Baird Of Elie, John Baird Of Lochwood, Alexander Baird Of Ury, James Baird Of Knoydart, Robert Baird Of Auchmedden, Douglas Baird Of Closeburn, George Baird of Strichen, David Baird Of Stichill.

Alexander leased a coalfield in 1816 which was run by his 20 year old son, William Baird. Eventually they took a long lease on Gartsherrie where they successfully sunk many pits. The Canal Company constructed a branch to two of the pits and the Garnkirk and Glasgow Railway opened in 1830. Coal could then either be delivered by canal or railway giving the Bairds a great advantage in the coal trade. In 1828, they began to erect the first iron furnace at Gartsherrie but eventually there were sixty blast furnaces there. Within six years the population near Gartsherrie rose to 26,000.

All the brothers except John, who remained a farmer, were partners in William Baird & Co. and they eventually ran six separate ironworks: Gartsherrie in Lanarkshire and Blair, Eglinton, Lugar, Muirkirk and Portland in Ayrshire and they made 300,000 tons of iron a year. Alexander Baird died at his farm in 1833 and his widow died in 1851. James Baird, was the last to be involved with the company.

Robert Baird who is buried here, studied law, and received a better education than his brothers. He completed his degree but practiced law briefly in Glasgow. The business of William Baird & Company had become so extensive that he was made a partner in the firm. At first he took charge of a colliery at Thankerton but soon was transferred to the office in Glasgow to take charge there. In 1854 he purchased the estate of Auchmedden, in order to buy back an estate which in the past had belonged to the Baird family. He was a Deputy Governor of the Forth and Clyde Canal, and, at the time of his death in 1856, he held the office of Lord Dean of Guild of Glasgow.

ROBERT STEWART OF MURDOSTOUN AND LANGBYRES 1810-1866
Designed by architect James Brown
Sculptor McLean
Omega Division

Born in Glasgow in 1810 Robert Stewart trained in accountancy. On his father's death he took over his position of iron and coal master at Omoa on the estate of Cleland. He reconstructed the works, took on a lease of a mineral field and discovered a seam of blackband ironstone which led to him making his fortune.

He joined the Glasgow Town Council in 1842 and took up a series of posts: River Bailie in 1843, Magistrate in 1845 and Senior Bailie or Chief Magistrate in 1847 and he was active, 'on horseback and in his office', in suppressing civil disturbances. In 1852 he married Isabella King, daughter of King of Levernholme and they had one daughter and two sons. In 1851, when he was Lord Provost he concentrated on the task of obtaining a clean water supply from Loch Katrine for Glasgow. There was real opposition to the plan but he persevered.

The Water Bill was carried through in 1855 and the works completed in 1859 - one of the great achievements for Glasgow. He retired from the council in 1855 and a year later, acquired the estate of Murdostoun for sum of £55,000, to which he added the lands of Langbyres, situated close by in 1865. He died suddenly in 1866 of heart disease aged 56.

The fountain in Kelvingrove Park, designed by James Sellars with sculpture by Mossman, which commemorates the bringing of water to Glasgow, has a portrait of him on the main central strut.

JAMES SCOTT 1810-1884
Omega Division

Born in Glasgow in 1810 he joined the calico printers of James, Black and Co at the age of sixteen and became a partner four years later. From 1835 he took an interest in the railways but retired from business in 1847 at the age of 37.

He married Jane Galbraith in 1848 and they had five sons and five daughters. A few years after he retired he returned to establish what became Scotland's largest cotton spinning firm, and in 1856 also rejoined his old firm.

In 1871 he took an interest in the oil industry and erected works over mineral fields in Renfrewshire and Pentland. He was on the Glasgow Town Council from 1846 to 1855 during the inception of the Loch Katrine water supply and the formation of Public Parks, Museums, and Art Galleries, including the formation of Kelvingrove Park. He also served as a Justice of the Peace and he died in 1884 aged 74 and was survived by eight of his ten children.

JAMES SCOTT AND FAMILY DIED 1850
Omega Division

Inscription:

In memory of James Scott, merchant of Montreal, aged 55; Lillias Ure, his wife aged 46; and Marion, their only child, aged 7; also of Janet Ure aged 40, sister of Mrs Scott and relict of William Smith, merchant, Montreal: who all perished in the wreck of the steamship, Orion, off Port Patrick, 18th June 1850, and are here intered; except the child Marion whose body was not found.

The family of James and Lillias Scott and daughter Marion were returning from Montreal, Canada, to make their home in Glasgow. Lillias' sister Janet and her husband William came with them to help them and see them settled.

They were all on board the Orion, an iron steamship that ran from Liverpool to Glasgow. She ran aground just off Port Patrick in calm weather when she came too close in to shore and struck a rock. She sank in 10 minutes killing 47 people out of the 200 on board including the crew.

This family were buried in the Glasgow Necropolis, other families were buried in Sighthill Cemetery and some of the crew of the vessel are buried in the Southern Necropolis.

The Captain and first mate were tried for negligence and imprisoned.

ERECTED
IN MEMORY OF
JAMES REDDIE
ADVOCATE
BORN AT DYSART, NOV. 22. 1775.
DIED AT GLASGOW. APRIL 8. 1852
HIS DAUGHTER-IN-LAW
MARGARET CLELAND BURNS
WIFE OF CHARLES REDDIE,
WHO DIED SEPT 26. 1924.
AGED 69 YEARS.
HIS GRANDSON
JAMES GEORGE REDDIE
ELDEST CHILD OF
MAJOR C. E. REDDIE, H. E. I. C. S.
WHO DIED DEC. 8. 1857,
AGED 10 YEARS.
HIS SON
JAMES CAMPBELL,
BORN NOV. 26. 1807, DIED JULY 4. 1879.
HIS SON
CHARLES,
BORN APRIL 12. 1810, DIED OCTOBER 12. 1889.

"I KNOW THAT MY REDEEMER LIVETH"

JAMES REDDIE MONUMENT 1775-1852
Omega Division

One of the most eminent lawyers of his time. Born in Dysart in Fife in 1775 and from a 'respectable' family he was educated at the High School in Edinburgh.

Edinburgh at that time was known as 'The Athens of the North' and he associated at school with many who became respected literary names. Despite his interest in literature himself he pursued his career in law and qualified as an advocate in 1797.

In 1804 he was proposed and accepted as Town Clerk, Assessor of Magistrates and Presiding Judge in Glasgow.

He had a broad legal knowledge but he concentrated in International Maritime Law and after a long career he retired from active life in 1822 to concentrate on producing many books based on his experiences especially relating to Maritime Law. He died in 1852 aged 77 after a long illness. He had several children one of whom also became a Judge.

DAVID ROBERTSON 1795-1854
Designed by architect James Hamilton
Sculptor Clubb and McLean
Epsilon Division

Born in 1795 in Monteith, Perthshire his father was a
farmer. He came to Glasgow at the age of fifteen and
worked with the Bookseller William Turnbull in his
premises in Trongate.

On the death of Mr Turnbull he took over the business
along with Thomas Atkinson (see page 55) as a partner.
They went their separate ways seven years later and over
the years he published a great deal of William Motherwell's
(see page 28) work and that of Alexander (Sandie) Rodger
(see page 131). He died of cholera in 1854 and his son
carried on his business in the Trongate.

He was also a patron of one of Glasgow's most famous
pedlars, William Cameron - 'Hawkie' who was born in
Stirlingshire, in the 1790s. Lame through a childhood accident, he was first apprenticed to a tailor but gave it up
to become an evangelical field preacher. Inspired by the
success of other street showmen, he began to sell 'speech-
es' and other cheap print after his arrival in Glasgow in
1818. Hawkie wrote his own pieces and performed on his
home patch of Glasgow High Street and the Trongate and
an example of Hawkie's street 'patter' was recorded by the
poet William Finlay. In the 1840s he spent increasing
amounts of time in prison or hospital, occasioned by his
chronic alcoholism and during that time he wrote his own
autobiography at the request of his patron, David
Robertson. He died in the Glasgow Poorhouse in 1851.
The autobiography was printed in 1888 and he had a
statue created in his honour by sculptor William Gemmell
which can still be seen at Pillar House in Eaglesham.

ROBERT KETTLE 1791-1852
Sculptor J and G Mossman
Epsilon Division

Robert Kettle was born in 1791 in a small cottage in the Ochil hills. His parents were very religious crofters and, although he wanted to enter the church, his parents did not have the money so he became apprenticed to a weaver.

His mother died when he was fourteen years old and at the age of seventeen he had a life threatening fever from which no one thought he would recover. When he was twenty four he moved to Glasgow and became a clerk in a cotton trade house.

Through his attendance at church he became a deacon and eventually set up a Sabbath School. His life was quite settled until 1829 when the cotton house he worked for failed and he nearly lost all his savings.

He had enough however to set up his own business as a cotton yarn merchant and he was extremely successful giving half of his income to the poor. It was at this time he became involved with the Temperance movement.

Initially it was set up to promote abstainance from 'distilled liquor' but from 1832 total abstainance was required. He admitted that he did have some difficulty with this as he enjoyed his glass of wine but eventually gave it up and became President of the Scottish Temperance League.

He died suddenly aged 61 and 2000 people attended his funeral in the Necropolis. A memoir of his life was written by William Reid in 1853.

THE TEMPERANCE MOVEMENT

In 1829, Mr. John Dunlop, Greenock, formed a Temperance Society at Maryhill and The Glasgow and West of Scotland Temperance Society was also established later in the same year. Both organisations asked their members to abstain from spirits, but allowed wine and beer. By 1830 several local societies existed with a membership of about 5,000. A year later there were fourteen societies in Glasgow with 8,000 members.

In 1832, the Tradeston Total Abstinence Society was formed and a large number of the members of the temperance movement joined. A year later representatives from thirty societies, met in Glasgow and formed The Scottish Temperance Union.

In 1844, the National organisation, The Scottish Temperance League, was formed at Falkirk with a membership of 12,000 and its headquarters in Glasgow. It soon attracted many who had been connected with the Union.

In 1854, the Glasgow Abstainers' Union was formed. For forty years it provided cheap concerts, morning coffee stands, a sea side convalescent home for the poor, bands of hope and penny savings banks.

In 1856, the Scottish Prohibition Society for the Suppression of the Sale of Intoxicating Liquor by Legal Enactment was established. The Society continued till the formation of The Scottish Permissive Bill and Temperance Association which joined with the United Kingdom Alliance to secure the prohibition of liquor.

At this time the Independent Order of Good Templars was formed in America. They sent a 'Scotchman, Mr. Thomas Roberts, to institute the Order in his native land'. The object of Good Templary is the absolute prohibition of the manufacture, importation, and sale of all intoxicating liquors to be used as a beverage. In November, 1870, a Band of Hope Union was formed in Glasgow and provided entertainment as an 'effective counter attraction to the licensed public houses'.

Meanwhile the Licensing (Scotland) Act of 1853 had limited the hours of opening for licensed premises. They were closed on Sundays and at 11pm on weekdays but temperance reformers wanted more extensive legislation. In 1890, Glasgow Corporation, passed a resolution that no more licensed premises would be allowed on Corporation property and there was strong political support for temperance reform in Scotland. There was also strong support for the introduction of legislation aimed at establishing the right of householders in local communities to vote for or against licensed premises. Scottish Local Option Bills in 1899, 1900 and 1905, were defeated because they were seen as having been influenced by American prohibition. However, The Temperance (Scotland) Act became law in 1913 and was put into force at the end of the 1914-1918 World War. Under this legislation local authorities asked electors to vote for either a no-change resolution, a limiting resolution, or a no-licence resolution. When the first Scottish Local Veto Polls were taken in 1920, more than forty districts voted for a no-licence resolution. This resulted in some licences which had already been granted in these districts being removed. The wartime licensing laws stayed in force until 1976. 2007 sees major reforms proposed which will replace Scotland's 30-year old licensing laws. New local licensing boards will look at complaints from local residents about pubs when considering licence applications and give them the power to decide drinking time on a pub-by-pub basis, removing Scotland's closing hour of 11pm. **89**

STEVENSON STEWART
Epsilon Division

This monument is to Alexander Bannatyne Stewart who
died in 1880, his wife Fanny Stevenson who died in 1913
and their son John Stevenson Stewart who died in 1898

PETER STEWART 1860-1887
Sculptor James Pittendrigh Macgillivray

Profile of the deceased with a greek classical figure
placing a laurel branch on a sacophagus

JOHN STRANG 1795-1863
Made by J. & G. Mossman
Epsilon Division

John Strang was born and educated in Glasgow and spent his life chiefly in literary and artistic pursuits.

He succeeded his father, John Strang, of Dowanhill in his wine business but had also inherited a little money from him so decided to go to France, Italy and Germany to study languages, literature and art. When he returned to Glasgow he translated and published French and German authors and in 1832 he edited 'The Day', a short-lived daily paper.

His book "Necropolis Glasguensis; with observations on ancient and modern tombs and sepulture", published in 1831, was the document he presented to the Merchants' House to persuade them to convert Fir Park into a garden cemetery like Pere la Chaise. He had visited this garden cemetery on his travels and it was a cause very close to his heart.

In 1834 he became Chamberlain of Glasgow and in 1842 Strang married Elizabeth Anderson. He wrote his most interesting book published in 1853, "Glasgow and its Clubs," which tells a lot about the manners and customs of Glasgow at that time.

His last work called 'Travelling Notes of an Invalid in Search of Health' was published a few days before his death. He had already asked if the Merchants' House 'would grant me and my wife a small, last resting place as a recognition of my labours connected with the cemetery from 1827-1833' which they did. He died childless in 1863.

THE PROFESSORS OF GLASGOW UNIVERSITY

Glasgow College, which later became Glasgow University, was established in the High Street in 1460.

The Professors who taught at Glasgow Universtiy and their families were allowed to be buried in the Blackfriars church which stood to the south of the University buildings shown on the right in the image below.

However the University sold the land to a Railway Company for a considerable sum and moved to Gilmourhill in the west end of the city in 1870.

Blackfriars church was demolished in 1876 and the incumbents of the graveyard were exhumed and reburied here in the Necropolis.

ROBERT COCHRAN
BORN 27TH SEP 1839, DIED 20TH MAY 1907.
MARY MAUD, HIS DAUGHTER
BORN 17TH SEP. 1871, DIED 28TH JULY 1903.
GRISELDA WILSON HOGG, HIS WIFE
BORN 30TH MARCH 1848, DIED 12TH MARCH 1932.
ROBERT CONRAD, HIS SON
BORN 14TH MAY 1873, DIED 18TH SEP. 1937.

ROBERT COCHRAN

ROBERT COCHRAN 1839-1907
Epsilon Division

The stone at the front is for one of his daughters and her family.

Robert Cochran was born in 1839 and was one of a
consortium who bought the Glasgow and Verreville Glass
and Pottery Company in Finnieston, Glasgow, in 1864. He
married Griselda Wilson Hogg and they had two sons and
two daughters and Robert died aged 68 in 1907.

The Verreville Glass Works was established in 1776. Workmen were
brought from England and Germany to build the cone which at 120 feet
high was a Glasgow landmark. Manager John Geddes, a former manager,
bought Verreville in 1806 and constructed a pottery and the glassworks and
pottery operated side by side. The 'Glasgow and Verreville Glass and Pottery
Company' was the largest industrial pottery of its time exporting to North
America and Ireland. Geddes and his wife, Christian Robertson, lived in
Verreville House adjacent to the works.

In 1830 Geddes became bankrupt and the pottery was taken over by
another former manager, Robert Montgomery. In 1833 he also became
bankrupt and the glassworks were closed in 1834.

Robert Alexander Kidston, a partner in the Anderston Pottery (or Lancefield
Pottery) then bought the house and works. Kidston added the production of
porcelain but by 1841 was in financial trouble. The firm changed hands
several times until finally, in 1864, Robert Cochran, with a consortium of
other businessmen, procured the Verreville and it remained a family
business until it was sold in 1918.

Grace Street originally ran between Stobcross Street and Finnieston Street
and was named after Geddes' daughter, Grace, who died from burns after
her dress caught fire while dressing for a party.

JAMES TEMPLETON 1802-1885
Epsilon Division

James Templeton was born in Paisley in 1802 and was
originally a shawl weaver who brought some of his weaving
ideas to carpets. By 1839 he had invented a new process
that made an increased colour range in carpet designs
available.

He was originally based in an old factory near Glasgow
Green but as he progressed he decided he wanted to build
a new factory. He asked architect, Sir William Leiper, to
design a building based on what James Templeton considered to be one of the most beautiful buildings in the world,
the Doges Palace in Venice. Work started on the Templeton
Carpet Factory in 1889 and it was completed by 1892.
Additions have been made to the building and the one
completed in the 1930s is a good example of the art deco
style of that period.

The factory produced carpets for two British Coronations,
a White House carpet, carpets for luxury liners and even
army blankets during the First World War.

The Templeton factory closed in 1982 and is now the
Templeton Business Centre and residential development.

JOHN SINCLAIR TEMPLETON d1918
Epsilon Division

There have been several attempts by thieves to remove the bronze 'lid'
and it is now in storage.

This monument details the deaths of his three wives who
all died young. Mary Stephen, married in 1859 died in
1863 aged 26, Emily Jane Fraser Campbell, married in
1877 and died in 1878 aged 25 and Mary Zelinda
Glennie, married in 1885 and died in 1887 aged 33.

STEPHENS OF LINTHOUSE
Epsilon Division

This shipbuilding company was established in 1750 and they built mainly on the East coast of Scotland until, in 1851, one half of the business was transferred to the Clyde finally moving to Linthouse, Glasgow, in 1869.

The company had specialised in sailing vessels, with some steamships and in 1871 they built an engine works and concentrated on cargo-passenger vessels of which the first four were for the Clan LIne.

By 1886 they had built 193 ships and in 1904 the 'Virginia' for the Allan Line was one of the first turbine driven Atlantic steamers.

When Alexander Sen retired, his sons became controlling partners, their uncle, John Stephen, remaining chairman and F J Stephen ran the shipbuilding department.
In 1900 they became Alexander Stephen & Son Ltd.
The company then began to concentrate on building higher class cargo liners and passenger vessels and later became involved in war production.

They were conscientious employers and set up a welfare department, facilities for sport and recreation and the Stephen Apprentices Boys Club. In 1932, the sixth generation in the form of Alexander Murray Stephen (1892-1974) took over as Chairman. Sir Murray Stephen retired in 1965. The shipbuilding assets and activities of Alexander Stephen & Sons Ltd were transferred to Upper Clyde Shipbuilders (UCS) in 1968 when the yard was closed to make way for the Clyde Tunnel. The engineering and ship repairing side remained in family hands until 1976.

A AND J INGLIS
Epsilon Division

Antony and John Inglis trained with *Tod and McGregor. Anthony began his working life as a bell hanger and general engineer in the Anderston district of Glasgow in 1840 and when his brother joined him they started building marine engines and boilers at the Whitehill Foundry. They moved into shipbuilding at the Pointhouse Yard near the mouth of the River Kelvin in 1862.

They built 53 ships before the first World War for The British India Steam Navigation Company which was a Glasgow company, and a total of 500 ships were built in its 100 year history. The company's reputation was based on its paddlesteamers which include The Waverley in 1946 and the Maid of the Loch in 1953 and the steam yachts, one of which was The Royal Yacht HMY Alexandria, built for Edward VII, in 1907.

The Pointhouse Yard was taken over by Harland and Wolff in 1919 and it was closed in 1965.

*Tod and McGregor – Builders of the ground breaking ocean-going iron screw ship, the City of Glasgow in 1850. David Tod and John McGregor were two of David Napier's sea going engineers and later foremen who set up their own engineering works when David Napier talked of moving his marine engineering business to London. David Napier's cousin was Robert Napier of Robert Napier and Sons, Govan and he was known as the 'Father of Clyde Shipbuilding'.

ROBERT BLACKIE.

W. G. BLACKIE

JOHN ALEXANDER BLACKIE 1850-1918
Designed by Talwin Morris.
The image is of a butterfly - a symbol representing resurrection
Epsilon Division

John Alexander Blackie (1850-1918), commemorated here along with his wife and son, was the eldest son of Walter G Blackie and grandson of the founder of Blackie and Son, the Publishing company. He was educated at Glasgow Academy, then at Cannstatt in Germany, and afterwards studied at Glasgow University. He received his first business training in the office of Alexander Moore, accountant, where he remained for three years before he entered his father's business of Blackie & Son, eventually becoming a partner in 1876. He travelled to America and Africa, and made several visits to Australia and New Zealand. He was married in Melbourne in 1855 to Sarah Gemmell and had a family of two daughters and one son.

THE PUBLISHING HOUSE OF BLACKIE

The founder of the Publishing house of Blackie was John Blackie senior, who was born in Glasgow in 1781. He went to work in the tobacco trade aged 6 and was apprenticed to a weaver aged 11. When his apprenticeship ended he spent two more years as a journeyman weaver, he then took employment in the weaving shop of John Duncan. In 1804 he married their daughter Catherine and had 3 sons - John junior, Walter G and Robert. John senior became employed as a bookseller eventually buying the business in 1808. In 1826 the eldest son John junior, joined the business, Blackie and Son. He went on to become Lord Provost of Glasgow from 1863 to 1866. Second son Walter G Blackie trained as a printer and took over a printing works which became known as W G Blackie and Co. This was a separate company until 1842 when W.G. Blackie and third son, Robert were made partners in Blackie & Son. Blackie's were the first publishing house to have their own art studio and it was Robert who appointed designer, Talwin Morris, in 1893 to run the studio. John Blackie senior died in 1874, John junior having died the previous year.

Walter G. Blackie's second son – Walter W Blackie also joined Blackie and Son and he was the one who commissioned The Hill House, designed by

FIRE SERVICE AND SALVAGE CORPS
Cheapside Street Fire 1960
Kilbirnie Street Fire 1972
Epsilon Division

In 1960, Arbuckle Smith and Co's Whisky bond in Cheapside Street, Glasgow, went on fire and at its height, 450 men were engaged in fighting a fire fuelled by more than a million gallons of whisky and rum that was in the bond and which sent fierce flames into the night sky. The walls of the warehouse were blown out into Cheapside Street and Warroch Street simultaneously as a result of an explosion inside the building and fourteen firemen and five men from the Glasgow Salvage Corps were buried under the masonry and died. It was Glasgow's worst peace-time disaster of the 20th century and it took a week to completely extinguish the fire.

On the south face of the monument is another inscription detailing the loss of life of seven firefighters in a fire, in 1972, at Sher Brothers' cash and carry warehouse in Kilbirnie Street, Glasgow. There were sixty firemen and twelve fire appliances at the site and the seven firemen died after one man was trapped inside the building and six of his colleagues attempted to rescue him.

The fire was thought to have been caused by a fluorescent light bulb which exploded causing a small fire. The owner and two workmen tried to put the fire out themselves but were unsuccessful and called the Fire Service.

HISTORY OF THE FIRE SERVICE

Before 1890 the firemen had little equipment and the procedures, on the outbreak of a fire, are described below.

Possession was taken of any horse, no matter how old or ill, and it was taken to Bell Street, where most of the members of the brigade lived. They were mainly shoemakers, slaters, and other craftsmen who also looked after the equipment which consisted of small ladders, axes, crowbars and pole hooks. The helmets were made of leather, latterly some being bound with brass, and the hoses were either canvas or riveted leather. On arrival at Bell Street the firemen were summoned by drum, the captured horse was attached to a cart and driven as fast as it could go. The water was taken from huge barrels, placed at intervals through the city, put into smaller barrels and transferred to the cart. When they reached the fire they did their best with the poor equipment and with the little water they had.

By 1890 Glasgow was the first in the UK to install electric street alarms and eventually alarm bells rang at firestations nearest the fire. There were 577 fires in the city in 1892 and the monetary loss was estimated at £120,000.

A description of procedures after 1890.

"All honour to the Boys of the Fire Brigade, who at risk of life and limb, are ever ready to fight the flames, and immortality to Braithwaite, who is credited with being the maker, if not the inventor, of the first steam fire-engine."

'The horses, beautiful animals, swift in running, well groomed and fed, by an automatic movement are set free from their stalls and of their own accord hasten from their stables, in a few moments are harnessed to the fire-engine, and in an incredibly short time are hastening towards the place where the flames are threatening to destroy both life and property, the shrill sounds of a whistle causing every vehicle and pedestrian to "clear the way." When the building on fire has been reached the firemen invade the premises, and ply their axes so as to reach the seat of the fire, while streams of water begin to play on every place where the enemy lurks, and the battle between fire and water begins, ending in the victory of the latter, although sometimes not until the victory is almost as bad as a defeat.'

On the monument:

THOMAS ANDREW MILLAR
BORN 3RD DECEMBER 1880
DIED 25TH JANUARY 1922
AND HIS BELOVED WIFE
MARY REID MORTON
BORN 22ND AUGUST 1881
DIED 9TH JULY 1948

THOMAS ANDREW MILLER 1880-1922
Sculptor William Kellock Brown

Another fine Angel.

THOMAS DUNLOP 1855-1938
Epsilon Division

Dunlop was a ship owner and business man. The eldest son of Thomas Dunlop (1831-1893), he was born in Glasgow in 1855. He was educated first at Glasgow Academy and then at Strathclyde University. He served an apprenticeship with one of the largest foreign merchant firms of the time before joining his father's business.

As well as grain merchants they were also shipowners, marine insurance brokers and Lloyd's agents and their fleet was the Queen Line of steamers and the Clan Line of sailing ships. Dunlop was also Consul for the Republic of Paraguay. In 1879 he married Miss Robina Mitchell, and they had a family of three sons and three daughters.

He was on Glasgow Town Council in 1901, Lord Provost (1914-1917), created a baronet in 1916 and appointed a GBE in 1918. His house was in Wemyss Bay as his chief pastime was yachting. As Director of the Royal Glasgow Institute of the Fine arts and Vice-President of Glasgow Art Club from 1906-1908. he had a fine collection of paintings of the Glasgow school.

His grandson and great grandson of the same name carried on the business until the 1980s.

IN EVER LIVING AND GLORIOUS MEMORY
OF
GEORGE LENNOX WATSON, M.I.N.A.
NAVAL ARCHITECT
DESIGNER OF HIS MAJESTY'S YACHT, Britannia
AND OVER FOUR HUNDRED RACING,
CRUISING AND STEAM YACHTS,
ELDEST SON OF THOMAS WATSON, M.D.
AND GRANDSON OF
GEORGE WATSON, SURGEON GLASGOW
WHO WAS CALLED TO REST
IN THE MIDST OF HIS LIFE-WORK
ON SATURDAY THE 12TH NOVEMBER 1904.

JUSTICE TO THE LINE AND EQUITY TO THE PLUMMET

GEORGE LENNOX WATSON 1851-1904
Primus Division

Naval Architect, George Lennox Watson was born in Glasgow in 1851. He was commissioned to design one of the most famous racing yachts of all time, The Royal Yacht 'Britannia', for the Prince of Wales and it was built and launched in Partick in 1893.

He also designed Lord Dunraven's 'Valkyrie II' which was beaten by the American *'Vigilant' in the 1893 America's Cup. Watson was given carte blanche to design 'Valkyrie ' for Lord Dunraven's second attempt at The Cup against the American 'Defender' in 1895. Dunraven lost and his allegation that the Americans had cheated put an end to his racing career. That yacht was broken up in 1901 and Watson died at the age of 53 in 1904.

Part of the inscription reads:

'Justice to the line and equity to the plummet'

'Vigilant' was beaten twelve times by Britannia in the Solent. Britannia is shown in the photograph below,

ADAMSON FAMILY
Sculptor William Scott
Primus Division

William Scott's other monument in the Necropolis is for Sam McCalden, which features a relief of a speedway rider and the inscription

'See you later glamour boy'
The stone itself dates from 1915.

This monument to the Adamson Family is a pink granite cross with anchor.

Alexander Adamson died in Chistlehurst, Kent, his wife, Margaret Murdoch MacCall, died in 1892 aged 44 and their only child Isobel aged five months died in 1874.

There was an architect called Alexander Adamson about whom little is known. This Edinburgh based man has been tentatively identified as the designer of the Gothic-style stonework of the Albert Bridge, the most richly ornamented bridge over Glasgow's River Clyde.

ROBERT DICK 1821-1891
AND JAMES DICK 1823-1902
OF GREENHEAD
Primus Division

Born of humble parents in Kilmarnock the family moved
to Glasgow in 1829. Robert was an inventor and came up
with a gum substitute to use instead of leather for soles of
shoes. James was commercially astute and the two brothers
set up their business, R. & J. Dick, in Greenhead, Glasgow.
From their office 'the workshop next door hummed and
thumped in the making of guttapercha soles for cheap
shoon'.

James eventually left the partnership, married a girl
from the Greenhead works and went to Australia where
he bought a share in both a silver and gold mine and
became a millionaire.

Robert died a bachelor aged 71 and although James
married he had no children. On his death in 1902
aged 79, the total estate left by James Dick was
£1,077,000. Half a million pounds was bequeathed
to charities all over Scotland.

The workers in the business received money gifts
that totalled £108,915. He handed over the
business of R. & J. Dick to his principal workers
and a substantial part of the residue was devoted
to the creation of a pension fund for the workers

HENRY HIGGINS 1848-1922
Primus Division

Henry Higgins was born in 1848, the son of Henry Higgins, warehouseman, and his wife Jane Murdoch Cameron. He served a five year architectural apprenticeship and subsequently acted as principal assistant for five years, of which at least the last two were spent in the Glasgow office of James Boucher.

In 1875 Boucher took him into partnership and the firm became Boucher & Higgins. In 1878 he married Jane Allan Campbell. His son G H Higgins joined the practice, but died sometime around 1892 after he designed Temple Church at Anniesland, Glasgow.

Higgins continued to practise alone after Boucher's death in 1906 and his practice consisted mainly of churches, houses and public schools in Glasgow, and surrounding districts. It was continued by another son, H E Higgins who was born in 1878. Both the father and his son lived in Bearsden, the father at Rosengarten and the son at Coila and the practice was based at 248 West George Street, Glasgow. Henry Higgins died of cancer at the age of 74 in 1922.

ERECTED
BY THE
SCOTTISH FOOTBALL
ASSOCIATION
In Memory Of
WILLIAM DICK
Who Died 10ᵀᴴ April 188
Aged 29 Years.

WILLIAM DICK 1862-1881
Sculptor George Galloway
Quartus Division

The sculpture illustrates the old fashioned laced football

This monument commemorates the first secretary of the SFA who died aged 29 after 10 years service. He was a referee and officiated at various matches.

The SFA was founded on 21 March 1872 following a meeting held in Dewar's Hotel, Glasgow, eight days earlier. The eight clubs who became founder members were as follows:

*3rd Lanarkshire Rifle Volunteers, Clydesdale, Dumbreck, Eastern, Granville, Kilmarnock, Queen's Park and Vale of Leven.

Queen's Park's extensive recreation ground was intended to meet demand from all kinds of sporting enthusiasts. It was here that Queen's Park, Scotland's oldest association football club, was founded in 1867 and they played here until their ground, Hampden Park, was opened in 1903.

The world's first football international was played in Glasgow in 1872, when Scotland and England played out a 0-0 draw but Scotland was one of the early founders of the game of football and its history stretches back well before 1872.

*In 1839 the threat of a French invasion led to the formation of groups of volunteer soldiers. By 1890 50,000 men in Scotland had volunteered and the first in Glasgow was the Third Lanarkshire Volunteer Rifle Corps who formed a regimental football team. They eventually became a battalion of the Cameronians (Scottish Rifles) TA.

WILLIAM DOLEMAN 1838-1918
Quartus Division

The winged sun at the top of the stone is another symbol of resurrection.

The four Doleman brothers who lived at 7, High Street, North Esk near Musselburgh were associated with golf for over 70 years.

William (1838-1918) was the best player and was the first amateur to enter the Open Championship.

A. H. Doleman (1836-1914) was one of the pioneers of golf in England and founder of golf at Lytham and St Annes.

John Doleman (1826-1918) the eldest, introduced the game to Nottinghamshire

Frank Doleman (1848-1929) was a clubmaker at Bruntsfield Links.

William Doleman is also credited as the first to play golf in Canada in 1854. As a sixteen year old sailor he went ashore from a military vessel and played a game on the Plains of Abraham, Quebec with golf clubs he had brought with him on the voyage.

This monument was erected by The Glasgow Golf Club who began playing in 1787 at Glasgow Green and a clubhouse was built there in 1792. A match in those days consisted of three rounds of the seven hole course. The Club folded during the 1830s, was reconstituted at Queen's Park between 1870 and 1875 and then moved back east, to a course at the then new Alexandra Park. The Glasgow Golf Club is now based at Killermont and operates a links course in Irvine.

GEORGE MASON 1838-1901
Sculptor Archibald Macfarlane Shannan
Quartus Division

Design of the lettering is similar to the Macintosh stone for McCall.
There are a number of stones in the Necropolis that are attributed
to Mackintosh from the time he was at Honeyman and Keppie.

George Mason was a photographic merchant and his wife,
Mary Cranston (1846-1932), was the cousin and close
friend of the famous Catherine (Kate) Cranston of the
Willow Tearooms which were designed by Charles Rennie
Mackintosh.

Mary Cranston's father, Bailie Robert Cranston, was the first
to finance Kate in her ambitions. He was an early supporter
of women's suffrage and educated both his daughters. His
wife was a full partner in their own hotel and in his daughter Mary he recognised the same ability. For her wedding
present he gave her the Washington Temperance Hotel in
Sauchiehall Street later named the Waverly Temperance
Hotel after her parent's hotel in Buchanan Street of that
name was sold.

MARGARET MCDOUGALL 1858-1904
The small monument missing a
top section facing the Mason
monument was erected by 'Mrs
Mason and their sorrowing family' and commemorates 'Margaret
McDougal, for 31 years the
faithful nurse and friend of the
late George Mason and Mrs
Mason'.

JOHN BELL 1823-1856
Quartus Division

John Bell was a house factor and was born in Gourock in 1823 as it states on the stone.

There is a symbol of a heart with three bells under the music - I have come across a reference to a Mr John Bell who in 1850, along with two friends, also called John Bell, had built to order the largest iron ship then afloat. It was named The Three Bells. I wonder if he may have been one of the three John Bells?

The inscription is taken from a song whose author is anonymous and reads :

Angels beckon me to the Land of the Leal

The section of the song is :

Dry your glistin' ee John
My soul langs tae be free John
The Angels wait for me
In the Land o' the Leal

In some versions of the song the words were changed to Jean not John - in an attempt to associate the song with Burns on his death bed saying farewell to his wife Jean Armour.

THOMAS BINNIE 1792-1867
Theta Division

Born at Nether Lauchope in 1792, Binnie came from farming stock and was described as follows:

'On his father's side, his ancestors had all been big men, and he was no degenerate scion. To the day of his death there were few men in Glasgow of a more imposing appearance; six feet three in height, with a singularly wide and deep chest, he gave one a most vivid impression of power.'

In 1819 he started working for himself as a builder and soon got a good reputation, walking for many hours to inspect sites and to spend time with his subcontractors.

The building trade was busier in Glasgow during the ten years from 1820 to 1830 than it had ever been before due to the increase in population. Binnie became mainly associated with construction in the east end and on the south side of Glasgow, in the Hutchesontown and Laurieston areas of the Gorbals.

He had an interest in philanthropy, becoming involved in schemes for temperance and black emancipation. He was a member of the Reformed Presbyterian Church and one of his two sons, Dr William Binnie, became a Professor of Church History in the Free Church College of Aberdeen. His other son, Thomas Binnie, became a successful property valuer in Glasgow.

DAVID PRINCE MILLER
Sculptor George Edwin Ewing
The sculptor of the Robert Burns statue in George Square
Eta Division

The inscription is very faint now but this monument is to David Prince Miller who was an actor in one of the 'Penny Geggie' shows, billed as 'the fastest shows on earth', which were usually abbreviated versions of the works of Shakespeare and short plays.

He could perform as many as four shows in one evening and made quite a good living. He paid for the erection of this monument himself and the bust is twice life size. Larger than life in reality and in death. His daughter is also buried here.

The most famous Pennie Geggie in Glasgow was in *Mumford's Theatre or Mumford's Geggie.

*Mumford's Geggie (gegg is an old Scots word for a show). It was the most famous of the Penny Geggies that were built in the city during the 19th century to provide cheap entertainment for working people.

Englishman William Mumford owned and managed the theatre from 1834 until about 1843, and it continued as a theatre until it became a clothes shop in the 1870s before being demolished in 1902.

HUGH TENNENT
1780-1864
CHARLES STUART PARKER TENNENT
1817-1864
Upsilon Division

Tennents with an 'e' is the Brewery family. The Tennent family had been connected with brewing in Glasgow since 1605 but the present site at Wellpark in the east end of Glasgow was acquired in 1777.

Hugh Tennent was born at Well Park in 1780. He began his working life as a manufacturer but took over the brewery in 1827 on the death of his uncle, John Tennent, broadening the solely domestic-market firm into an international concern. Hugh Tennent married Christian Rainy and they had five sons and two daughters. He had a love of sailing and he crossed the Atlantic in his schooner St Ursula. He died on board off Bantry Bay in 1864.

His youngest and fifth son Charles took over from his father in 1855 and further expanded the business to become the largest exporter of beer in the world. Charles died aged 47 five months before his father. In 1885 the brewery included a staff of 500, 40 Clydesdale horses and, at the end of each brewing season, a stockpile of 1,000,000 gallons of stout stored in 19,000-gallon vats. Two-thirds of this was exported in bottles. The Brewery is seen on the south boundary of the Necropolis. Not to be confused with the other Tennant family (chemical works) spelt with an 'a'.

Between these two monuments is the unmarked grave of architect John Honeyman who died virtually penniless in 1914.

BOTTLED BEER

The Cubans liked Tennent's Export Beer but preferred stoneware bottles. In 1915 Tennent's of Wellpark Brewery, Glasgow, found themselves in such a difficult position obtaining stoneware bottles that they decided to take over a pottery. They chose the Possil Pottery in north Glasgow and in 1920 the Pottery was purchased for £8,000.

Almost immediately after the Pottery was purchased disaster struck. Owing to speculation in sugar there had been a run on one of the smaller banks which had the Cuban government declare that money was no longer allowed to leave the country. Tennent's had beer on the way to Cuba from London and more at Glasgow and Hull waiting to go. The demand for Tennent's beer in Cuba never really recovered which meant that the demand for stoneware bottles diminished.

In 1921 the Coal Strike closed down many works but Tennent's transferred the Possil Pottery reserves of coal to the Wellpark Brewery where they were used to keep the cold storage plant running all through the strike. By 1924 the demand for Brewery bottles had increased again and 1925 the Pottery had a turnover of £70,000. 1926 was the year of the General Strike and the Pottery was immediately closed again.

It opened again but the next few years were difficult and all potteries were doing badly. Now glass bottles were considered more 'sanitary'. The Caledonian Pottery in Rutherglen had closed and during 1929 the Barrowfield Pottery in Glasgow's East End disappeared. Only three stoneware potteries were left in Scotland: Govancroft, Buchan's of Portobello and the Possil Pottery.

Over the years The Possil Pottery had saved the Company £22,000 and helped through the strikes. It struggled on until 1942 but it wasn't able to be sold as a going concern so they sold the building and a small amount of plant. The Company carried on purely as a holding company until the 1960s when it was then wound up.

Tennents Wellpark Brewery however is still going strong and the company was one of the first businesses in the United Kingdom to can beer and claims to have the largest sales of all beers sold in Scotland.

ALEXANDER MACKENZIE
d1875
Epsilon Division
Designed by
George Smith,
Sun Foundry.
Cast iron Gothic
monument.

ANNA STEPHEN
1812-1867
Sculptor Alexander MacDonald & Co
The cross was erected by
her son Reverend
Robert Stephen.

ALEXANDER SCOTT
1837-1911

This memorial was erected by
Alexander Scott to his wife
Catherine Lister who died in
November 1861 aged 25 and his
daughter Eliza McDowall who died
a year later in December 1862.

FRANCOISE FOUCART 1781-1863
Upsilon Division

Francoise Foucart was Officer of the Imperial Guard of France, Knight of the Legion of Honour and Professor of Fencing at the Royal Academy of Paris. Born in 1781, he spent 40 years in Glasgow as a fencing teacher and his pupils erected this monument to him.

Francoise Foucart was in London the day that Sir Robert Peel was thrown from his horse while riding up Constitution Hill in 1850. Foucart went to his assistance but the Prime Minister died three days later from his injuries.

PEEL STREET - named in honour of Sir Robert Peel, who passed the Reform Bill of 1832. From his name originated the title of "peeler," as applied to the police.

ALEXANDER BUCHANAN 1829-1850
Gamma Division

He is actually buried with other members of the Buchanan family a short distance from this monument.

To the memory of Alexander Buchanan born in 1829 who was a merchant in Glasgow and died at the age of 31. His wife, Jane Helen Simpson, is also remembered here and she lived to the age of 72.

PETER LAWRENCE 1796-1839
Sculptor J Mossman
Gamma Division

Peter Lawrence was one of the sculptors producing monuments for the Necropolis when it first opened and his many monuments include Anne Ritchie, the Crawford family, Patrick Graham and Andrew Gilbert, the father of artist John Graham Gilbert (see page 16). There was a design competition for this monument which was won by John Mossman. The winged youth representing Life, held an inverted, lit torch, the remains of which you can still see beside the foot. This work established John Mossman's reputation and you can see his work throughout the Necropolis. The detail below shows the foot.

He died in 1839 aged 43.
The inscription reads:

In Memory Of Peter Lawrence, Sculptor. Who Died 27th January, 1839. Age 43. A Few Friends Have Raised This Monument To Express Their Esteem And Admiration For His Worth As A Man And His Talent As An Artist. 1840.

MATHEW MONTGOMERIE 1782-1856
Designed by architect Charles Wilson
Sculptor Mossman - Figures Hope and Resignation
Monument by Hamilton and Miller
Gamma Division

Another Gothic monument - this one is based on Henry VII's chapel at
Westminster. The figures of Hope and Resignation are missing.

This monument was erected by Mathew Montgomerie,
a writer who was born in Irvine in 1782, and it
commemorates his wife Margaret Fleming. It was damaged
by a storm in 1856 shortly after it was built

DILETTANTE SOCIETY MAUSOLEUM
Designed by architect David Hamilton,
Gamma Division

David Hamilton was one of the members of the Society but is buried in the new Cathedral graveyard

The idea for this club "an association of artists, amateurs, and connoisseurs" originated with two Glasgow artists, David Mackenzie who died a poor man, in the 'Old Man's Institution' and J. A. Hutchison who was drawing master in the Old High School.

In September, 1828, the directors of the Glasgow Dilettanti Society opened their first exhibition in their Rooms in Argyle Arcade with an exhbition by living artists.

These rooms were where the designs for the Necropolis were exhibited in 1831. The society continued there till 1832 when they then moved to premises two stairs up at 51 Buchanan Street which proved not to be a popular location. In 1838 they held the eleventh and last exhibition for charity. About 1839, some art students asked to use the space and the society gave them the use of its library and its fine collection of 'casts from the antique'. The very last exhibition was of old masters and some modern works which had appeared at former Dilettanti exhibitions. There were 353 works lent by some 53 owners including Queen Victoria and Prince Albert.

Only two members of the society are buried here - Andrew Henderson, an eccentric, artist and chairman and Dr William Young a physician and vice chairman of the Society. Other members were Mr. Ewing of Strathleven, Archibald MacLellan, Mr. Smith of Jordanhill, Robert and William Towers, Charles Hutchison, John Houldsworth, William Euing, J. Oswald Anderson, Dr. Drury, David Hamilton, the architect, D. C. Rait, Thomas Atkinson, the bookseller and politician, and James and Robert Hart, "the scientific brothers,"

Strathclyde University hold the Society's collection.

The rooms continued to be called "The Dilettanti Rooms" for many years after the society itself was extinct.

AITKEN OF DALMOAK MAUSOLEUM
Designed by architect James Hamilton
Gamma Division

This mausoleum is the largest in the cemetery - the inset shows what's left of the fine cast iron gates and sculpture.

The name of this land between Dumbarton and Renton is probably derived from Gaelic dail (= "field") and maybe an older form of muc (= "pig"). The name is spelt "Dalmowack" in Pont's late 16th century map, suggesting an extra syllable.

Dalmoak Castle, home of the Aitkens in Dumbarton, West Dunbartonshire, is more a castellated Gothic mansion house than a fortified castle. The present building was erected in 1869, although it is believed that a building has stood here since the mid-15th century. Currently a private nursing home, it has a five bay facade of coupled windows, a large stained glass window and battlemented parapets with a central tower rising behind.

LAURENCE HILL 1791-1872
Beta Division

Described in 1857 'On the west of the semicircle is a massive perforated
wall supported at intervals by 4 elegant vases' ... 'At each end of the wall,
North and South, is a handsome ornamental cast iron gate'. The poetry was
described as the 'ornamental tracery which forms the leaf of the gate' and
were from Logan's 'Paraphrases' - on the south gate and James Beattie's
poem 'Minstrel' on the north gate.

Born in 1791, Hill was educated in Edinburgh and
Lincolnshire before moving to Glasgow in 1812. He
entered his family's long-established legal practice here
and was the factor for Glasgow University from 1819-1872
receiving an honorary degree LL.D, although he was
actually a classical scholar.

He campaigned for improvements to roads and in 1832
promoted, unsuccessfully, the first bill for a Glasgow to
Edinburgh Railway and was involved with the Garnkirk to
St Rollox Railway, the first line in Scotland on which
locomotives were used.

He was instrumental in the formation of the Glasgow
Necropolis and his first wife Barbara Hopkirk was the third
burial in the Necropolis. She had thirteen children and died
at the age of forty. He later married Marion Hill, his cousin.

From 1835 he campaigned to improve the quality of the
Clyde by removing Glasgow sewage to the Ayrshire coast.
Hill retired from business in 1840 and subsequently lived
in Ayr, Edinburgh and in the New Forest. In 1856 he
returned to Glasgow, where he died in 1872 aged 81.

DAVIDSON OF RUCHILL MAUSOLEUM
Designed by architect J T Rochead
Sculptor Hamilton and Miller
Beta Division

This small Greek temple is built of Craigland's Quarry stone and measures
22 ft by 12 ft. The original bronze doors are lying flat just inside.
Below are vaulted tombs.

James Davidson was involved in the muslin trade and was
a partner of James and John Meikleham whose warehouse
was in Glassford Street, Glasgow. After their death
Davidson became a successful merchant himself and
bought the lands of Ruchill, Garrioch and Balgray.
He died in 1851.

The Council bought 53 acres of his estate from his son,
William James Davidson, for the construction
of Ruchill Park and Hospital in 1893 for £29,176 5s.

RUCHILL

Was originally Roughill, and in the seventeenth
century the property of the Peadies, who were at that time
a leading family in Glasgow, but since then has been held
successively by the Dreghorn, Dennistoun, and Dundas
families. It was acquired by purchase by James Davidson
but he later built a home in Wemyss Bay and lived there,
Ruchill House being rented by J. H. Young, a manufacturer
in Glasgow.

WILLIAM HARPER MINNOCH 1820-1883
Sculptor Clubb and MacLean
Mnema Division

William Harper Minnoch was born in 1820 of parents Alexander Minnoch and Susan Harper.

He was a partner in the firm of John Houldsworth & Co, (see page 69) merchants in Glasgow. He was also the fiance of the infamous Madeleine Smith (her grandfather was David Hamilton, architect). She was accused (not proven verdict) of poisoning her lover Pierre Emile L'Angelier who is buried in the Ramshorn cemetery in the Merchant City, Glasgow. Not surprisingly William did not subsequently marry Madeleine and a year after the trial he married Mary Aitken.

Madeleine moved to London and In 1861 'Lena' Smith married Pre-Raphaelite artist George Wardle and enjoyed London society. In Sachervell Sitwell's book 'Splendours and Miseries' it was stated that the painter Rossetti used her as a model for several paintings of Mary Magdalene. George and Lena had two children but separated in 1889.

By this time her son had already moved to America and she decided at the age of 70 to join him and his family there. She was still married to George Wardle until he died in 1910. Four years later she married again, a much younger man said to resemble Wiilliam Minnoch. She died in 1928 aged 93 and was buried under the name Lena Wardle Sheehy in Mount Hope Cemetery, Westchester County. During her time in America she refused a Hollywood offer to make a film of her life story.

CHARLES WILLIAM FRY 1838-1882
Iota Division

Born in 1838 in Alderbury, Wiltshire, England his birth name was William Charles Fry.

The inscription is a verse that Fry wrote:

The former things are past,
And ended is the strife,
I'm safe home at last!
I live an endless life!

A brick layer by trade as was his his father, Fry was a versatile musician who played the violin, cello, piano, cornet, and harmonium, and led an orchestra and band at the Wesleyan chapel in Alderbury.

He also helped the Christian Mission in Salisbury, and his family band accompanied Salvation Army founder, William Booth, in evangelism camps. He was the first band master of the Salvation Army.

He died in 1882 at Park Hall, Polmont, Stirling aged 44.

JAMES MITCHELL 1802-1873
Mnema Division

This was erected by James Mitchell and the
inscription below explains why:

'Erected by James Mitchell, Painter, Glasgow
To mark
the spot where stood the dwelling-place of his
Father and Grandfather
which was occupied by them for a period of forty-eight years
previous to the formation of this Necropolis
and is now chosen as
the final resting place of their descendants'

DR JOHN LAUDER 1807-1847
Mnema Division

Not far from the Mitchell monument is that of another man whose family had lived in this area of the Necropolis. Mr John Lauder, a surgeon in the Carlton district of Glasgow, died 1847 aged 40, and the monument has the following inscription:

This is the spot where stood the dwelling house of the Grandfather and Grandmother of Dr Lauder, 55 years ago, and which he chose for his resting place

ALEXANDER McCALL 1836-1888
Designed by architect Charles Rennie Mackintosh
Portrait panel Sculptor J Pittendrigh Macgillivray
Sculptor Peter Smith
Theta Division

Grey granite Iona cross with bronze portrait panel

Alexander McCall was Chief Constable of the Glasgow
police for eighteen years. He was appointed a Detective
Inspector in 1850, Assistant Superintendent in 1858 and
Superintendent of the Central District in 1862. He is most
famous for tracking down the forger John Henry Greatrex
and his assistant Jenny Weir, in New York, and bringing
them back to Glasgow for trial in 1866.

The forger was sentenced to 20 years penal servitude and
McCall was promoted to the post of Chief Constable in
1870. He is also credited with improving relations between
the policeman on the street and the general public, through
a programme of disciplinary reforms.

His gravestone, in the form of a Celtic cross, was designed
by Charles Rennie Mackintosh, whose policeman father,
William, had worked as McCall's assistant. This is one of
the earliest known works by Mackintosh who lived for
some time (1875-1892) in Dennistoun in a tenement in
Firpark Terrace, bordering the eastern boundary of the
Necropolis.

ALEXANDER 'SANDIE' RODGER
1784-1846
Sculptor J and G Mossman
Mnema Division

The inscription on the stone states that he was a man
'gifted with feeling, humour and fancy'.

Known as the 'Radical Poet' and described as 'A radical
weaver, comic poet and satirist who enjoyed embarrassing
polite company.' He was born in Midcalder in 1784.

He started writing poetry when working as a weaver and
music teacher in Bridgeton, Glasgow. In 1819 he became
sub-editor of The Spirit of the Union, a newspaper which
advocated radical political reform.

There was a lot of political agitation at the time which
culminated in the Radical Rising of 1820, and he spent
eleven days in prison on suspicion of publishing seditious
material.

His first of several collections of poems was published in
1821. His mainly short poems were written in the Scots
dialect and combined political satire with humour.

He 'disgusted' Sir Walter Scott in 1822 by the publication
of a parody of Sir Walter's own 'Carle now the King has
come'- on the visit of George IV to Edinburgh. Many of his
poems were set to music, with some, such as 'The
Mucking o' Geordie's Byre', having inspired more modern
versions. He died in 1846 aged 62.

He has been mentioned earlier in the book as being friends with other poets
and booksellers who are also buried in the Necropolis and having written a
famous poem about Colin Dunlop (see page 46).

JAMES ROBERT DENNISTOUN
1798-1851
Beta Division

The eldest son of James Dennistoun of Colgrain (see page 61), James Dennistoun's monument is next to the Pattison family enclosure and is also inscribed for his daughter Barbara Reid, who died in 1841 aged 6, his wife Barbara Wilson Macredie, who died in 1900 and their son, Vice Admiral Robert Peel Dennistoun who died in 1913 aged 78.

WILLIAM DENNISTOUN
OF KELVINGROVE 1800-1850
Sigma Division

THE PATTISON FAMILY ENCLOSURE
Beta Division

There is an elegant group of monuments to the Pattison family – one of the ones erected against the face of the rock has the following inscription along with the arms of the family;

In memory of John Pattison of Kelvingrove, merchant of Glasgow, who died 28th Dec 1807 aged 57 and his beloved wife Hope Margaret Moncrieff of the ancient family of Culfargie who died 3rd September 1833 aged 77.

The Merchants' House enabled the family to place Colonel Pattison's Monument near his father's tomb

LIEUTENANT-COLONEL ALEXANDER HOPE PATTISON MONUMENT
1787-1835 - Sculptor John Richie - He is portrayed as a full length figure with head uncovered and a martial cloak around him.

Pattison was the Commander in Chief of the Second West India Regiment and Commander of the troops in the Bahamas. He served for twenty eight years and died aged 48 in Nassau in 1835.

His nephew of the same name, but a Lieutenant, is also remembered here on the monument on the left with helmet and sword. Both died on the island of Nassau and are buried in the same tomb there.

His brother, Granville Sharp(e) Pattison, 1791-1851, was an anatomist and was accused of body-snatching - a charge found not proven. He founded departments of Anatomy in London and New York.

I have posted the full profiles and inscriptions on these monuments on The Friends of the Glasgow Necropolis website.
www.glasgownecropolis.org

BOLTON AND HIGGINBOTHAM ENCLOSURE
Beta Division

A Grotto created for these two related families from the Stirling area.

Bolton of Carbrook started out in life as
a sailor. At the age of fifteen he began working
in the British office of an East Indian house,
in which he rose from junior clerk to senior
partner. He became a Member of Parliament
and an eminent businessmen at Ker, Bolton
& Co., Glasgow.

For some years, he was chairman of the Chamber
of Commerce, a director of the Caledonian Railway,
and chairman of the Callander & Oban line.

Mr Bolton married Miss Higginbotham, daughter
of Samuel Higginbotham, 1798-1881,
who was an important cotton manufacturer
in Glasgow.

ESTHER COOPER d1851
Sculptors J & G Mossman
Beta Division

These figures of Hope and Resignation are some of the best sculpture in the Necropolis.

Esther Cooper was the daughter of Henry Ritchie Cooper of Ballindalloch and Mary Jane, the only surviving child of Gerald Butler of Wexfordshire.

Her father was born 1816 in Stirlingshire and was the second son of Samuel Cooper and Janet Ritchie,

Her grandmother Janet Ritchie was the daughter of Henry Ritchie, partner in the Thistle Bank, whose estate was Craigton - now part of Govan, Glasgow

BELL FAMILY MAUSOLEUM
Designed by architect JT Rochead
Beta Division

The monument is in the form of an Egyptian doorway. Rochead also designed their Mansion, North Park House which was home to BBC Scotland for 70 years until 2006.

John (1806-1880) and Matthew Perston Bell (1808-1870) were founders of Bell's Pottery - one of the most important potteries in the history of the Scottish industry. They opened the Glasgow Pottery in the early 1840s and the company became very successful, producing pottery for local and overseas markets.

Matthew died of apopolexy at the age of 61 in 1870 and John, a recluse, died intestate in 1880 at the age of 73 which caused immense problems. It took a year to realise his estate which eventually was calculated to be in the region of £357,323.00 with the pottery still making a profit of £1000 a month, a very large sum of money at the time.

The 'heir at law' was James Bell, possibly of Bell and Bain, (see page 51) who died in 1883 before he received the inheritance which then passed to his son William. There were also 25 cousins all with claims. The estate was not just the pottery but shares in various mines, a company in Rangoon, including a sawmill and tannery, and houses and tenements in Glasgow and Millport.

The company was sold as a going concern but it couldn't compete with English and Dutch pottery manufacturers and production at the Glasgow Pottery ended around 1911.

JOHN MACFARLANE 1797-1869
Designed by Mossman
Beta Division

The monument features the caduceus as would be expected on a monument of a medical man.

A highly esteemed Professor of Medicine at Glasgow University as described on the stone.

WILLIAM YORK 1799-1865
Beta Division

One of Glasgow's most successful builders in the mid 19th century, he set up his business about 1834.

Some of his important buildings include The Custom House in Clyde Street, Glasgow, which was built in 1839 and whose Royal Arms provoked a demonstration when they were erected on the building. The Bank of Scotland in Ingram Street, Glasgow, had the shield and colossal caryatids by sculptor A H Ritchie (see page 148) escorted by York from Edinburgh in 1849. The Queen's Rooms in La Belle Place feature's York's name on it together with those of the building's architect, Charles Wilson, and its sculptor, John Mossman.

He was also the contractor for the building of the *Victoria Bridge 1854. York died in 1865 aged 66.

*The 500 year old predecessor on the same site, Bishop's Bridge, had become too restrictive for the growing demands of traffic. A new 50ft wide five span masonry arch bridge was designed by engineer, James Walker, with foundations 19ft below those of the old bridge, and timber piles which were steam-driven a further 14ft below that. When the Victoria bridge opened in 1854, Glasgow had the widest bridges in Britain.

RIGHT HON. LORD KELVIN, G.C.V.O., M.A., LL.D., D.C.L., F.R.S., F.R.S.E., D.L.
Mnema Division

His grandfather was a Scottish Ulsterman, tenant farmer in County Down. His father, James Thomson, In 1832, was appointed Professor of Mathematics at Glasgow University and wrote many books including 'Thomson's Arithmetic' which was in universal use for generations. He died 12th January, 1849. Two of his sons, William and James became professors at Glasgow University.

At the age of ten, in 1834, William Thomson, (Lord Kelvin), and his brother James, went to Glasgow University. In 1841 he went to St. Peter's College Cambridge, and took his degree in 1845. At the incredibly early age of twenty two he was given the Chair of Natural Philosophy at Glasgow University which he then occupied for fifty three years.

He is mainly remembered for the laying of the telegraph cable across the Atlantic from Ireland to Newfoundland in 1866 for which he received a knighthood. On the jubilee of his professorship in 1896, a three day festival was held in his honour with two and a half thousand invited guests.

He married Margaret, daughter of Walter Crum (see page 45), of Thornliebank in 1852. She died in 1870, and four years later he married Frances-Anne Blandy.

After an illness of three weeks, Lord Kelvin died at his house, Netherhall, Largs, in 1907, and he was buried in Westminster Abbey but his name is also on this family monument.

THE MUIR FAMILY 1868
Beta Division

This family died in the wreck of the steamship Caronne off Lands End.

The Parents

James Muir aged 45

Mary (Erskine) Muir aged 36

The Children

Mary Erskine Muir aged 9

Margaret Elizabeth Muir aged 7

Anna Erskine Jackson Muir aged 9 months

SOME OF THE
ARCHITECTS,
SCULPTORS
AND FOUNDRIES
WHOSE WORK
IS IN THE NECROPOLIS

ARCHITECTS

SCULPTORS

FOUNDRIES

DAVID HAMILTON 1768-1843

Born in Glasgow in 1768 he trained as a stone-mason before becoming an architect and setting up his own business in 1790. His son James (1818–61) became his partner - David & James Hamilton and he contributed to many of the designs. Most of the banks they designed are now demolished. His apprentices, Thomas Gildard, Charles Wilson and J. T. Rochead amongst them, were treated as part of the family in the office/house. David Hamilton's work was highly thought of in his lifetime and Glasgow held a public dinner in his honour in 1840 at which he was presented with a gold casket containing £500. He died in 1843 from 'an attack of paralysis' and is commemorated in the new Cathedral Graveyard which is on the north side of the Cathedral.

WORK WITHIN THE NECROPOLIS

The cast iron Entrance Gates
Superintendent's House and Office
Bridge of Sighs
The Egyptian Vaults

OTHER WORK INCLUDES

Hutchesons' Hospital
Hamilton Palace
The Mausoleum for Alexander, the 10th Duke of Hamilton
Nelson Monument in Glasgow Green
Lennox Castle

CHARLES WILSON 1810-1863

The son of a builder and wool merchant, he was an apprentice in David Hamilton's office from 1827, becoming chief draughtsman in 1837.
He set up his own practice in 1839, producing some of Glasgow's finest buildings and mansions. He was central in the development of Glasgow's architecture and town planning in the mid-19th Century. He died in 1863 and was buried in the Southern Necropolis.

WORK WITHIN THE NECROPOLIS

Mathew Montgommerie Monument
Adam Paterson Monument
Alexander Craig Monument

OTHER WORK INCLUDES

Kirklee Terrace
Plans for the Botanic Gardens
Kelvingrove Park and Woodlands Hill
Park Circus
Sauchiehall Street
Southern Necropolis Gateway

Thomas Gildard's Recollections of David Hamilton

This article was by Thomas Gildard, who had been a pupil of David Hamilton's.

Gildard wrote, "in December 1838, I was apprenticed for five years with Messrs David & James Hamilton, whose office was at the head of Buchanan Street, on the site now occupied by the Langham Hotel. The house was a self-contained one of three stories, the first a few steps above the street. On the street floor, the office was to the right of the entrance lobby and Mr Hamilton's room to the left; and behind were kitchens, servant's quarters etc. Up one stair was a very handsome room which served the purpose of both dining-room and drawing-room; and a library of a somewhat unique plan which could be connected with it. Behind, and in the floor above were bedrooms.

"Mr Hamilton was in about his seventieth year, and was a man of most impressive presence, frank and kindly in manner, and with a bearing of easy dignity. He was what is commonly or conventionally called somewhat "aristocratic" in appearance, and in social intercourse was distinguished by much grace and courtesy. He was a man eminently to be looked up to. James, his son, who had not much more than attained his majority, was tall and remarkably handsome, his fine features somewhat of an Italian cast, and his long, glossy black hair rolling in ringlets.

"When I entered the office the late Mr Rochead had been in it six months a draughtsman and my friend, Mr Baird, a year or two. As the house and office were together, the lads, as we were called, were occasionally favoured by a visit from Mrs Hamilton and her daughters; indeed, Mrs Hamilton looked in almost every morning, took a seat, and had a kindly chat with us for half-an-hour or so. It seemed almost as if we were living "in family" and although it is a long time since, there remains with me a pleasant impression of the homely, hearty kindness that I experienced from all the Hamiltons under the old-fashioned arrangement of house and office together. Occasionally we dined in state with the family and sometimes we were favoured with a Saturday excursion to some important work in progress in the country.

"Mr Hamilton had formed an excellent library of not only great books on architecture but of books illustrative of painting and sculpture. He had also many choice line engravings and other things that might be expected in the house of a family all of inborn and suave and highly cultivated taste. He was the recognised head of the profession. His position was unique and as his fame had gone beyond, he had, I might almost say, frequent visits from men of eminence in the arts, bearing letters of introduction. I remember seeing Kemp, the architect of the Scott Monument, and Mr Hamilton bringing him down stairs to see the office.

"Mr James (Hamilton), Mr Rochead and Mr Baird were alike assiduous in the instructing of the apprentices; if there was a fault at all, it was in the apprentices being dealt with too much like pupils instead of being made immediately useful.

"The office hours were from nine till seven, the hour between four and five being the interval for dinner. On Saturdays the office closed at four. There was no gas in the office and, in the winter evenings we wrought by candlelight."

.

143

ALEXANDER 'GREEK' THOMSON
1817-1875

Born in Balfron, he trained as a lawyer's clerk before architect, Robert Foote, offered him an apprenticeship after seeing some of his drawings. In 1836, he joined the architectural practice of John Baird (Primus) and then established his own business in 1849 but formed a brief partnership with John Baird II from 1849-56. He set up A and G Thomson with his brother George in 1856 and became one of the first architect developers. He died in 1875 and was buried in the Southern Necropolis.

Although recognised in his own time as an architect of genius his work has been somewhat overlooked due to the attention given to Charles Rennie Mackintosh in Glasgow. However this is now being redressed due to the work of the Alexander Thomson Society.

WORK WITHIN THE NECROPOLIS

Beattie Monument
Inglis Monument
Many others are attributed to him

OTHER WORK INCLUDES

Caledonia Road UP Church
St Vincent Street UP Church
Grosvenor Building
Buck's Head Building
The Egyptian Halls
Mossmans' studio, North Frederick St
Queen's Park Terrace 1857-60 dem. 1980
Walmer Crescent 1857-62
Moray Place

THOMAS HAMILTON 1784-1858

Thomas Hamilton was born in Glasgow in 1784. His father, Thomas senior lived Edinburgh where he built a house at 166 High Street, which still stands today.

His business really took off when he won the competition to build the Burns Monument at Alloway in 1818. He died in 1858 and was buried in Calton Graveyard in the lair of his uncle, John Hamilton.

WORK WITHIN THE NECROPOLIS

The Doric column for the statue of John Knox 1825

OTHER WORK INCLUDES

Burns Monument at Alloway, Ayrshire
Dean Orphan Hospital, now Dean Gallery Edinburgh
Royal High School Edinburgh
King George IV Bridge Edinburgh
The College of Physicians Edinburgh

JOHN BAIRD (Primus) 1798-1859

Born in Dalmuir, Dunbartonshire, he trained as an architect with a relative, John Shepherd, of John Shepherd & Co, a firm of architects and property agents. In 1818, at the age of 20, he took over the business on Shepherd's death.

He pioneered the use of cast iron in his buildings the first of which was for the roof trusses in the Argyle Arcade in 1827 and then in 1856 Gardner's Warehouse. In conjunction with David Hamilton he was appointed to combine five competition designs for the Glasgow Necropolis into one. He died at his home in Partick in 1859, and was buried in Glasgow Necropolis in Sigma Division.

WORK WITHIN THE NECROPOLIS

James Ewing Monument

OTHER WORK INCLUDES

Prince of Wales Buildings (Princes Square)
Wellington Church, Wellington Street
Somerset Place, Sauchiehall Street
Claremont Terrace and Beresford House
Gardner's Warehouse
Argyle Arcade

JOHN BRYCE 1805-1851

John Bryce, born 1805, was the youngest of the three architect sons of William Bryce. The eldest son, William, worked in the office of William Burn but died in 1823 and his brother David inherited his place in that office. Nothing is known of John's training but it is assumed that he initially worked with his father and after that he was probably either in Burn's office or assisting David with his private practice.

However, by 1833, John was in Glasgow designing work within the Glasgow Necropolis. John Bryce died in 1851 at the age of 46 and was buried in Glasgow Necropolis. His son John, then very young, subsequently joined his uncle David's practice.

WORK WITHIN THE NECROPOLIS

The Jews' Enclosure
The McGavin Monument
The Façade

OTHER WORK INCLUDES

Duke Street Reformatory
North Woodside development
Bothwell Street development
Minerva Street, (now St Vincent Crescent) (attributed)
Corunna Street (attributed)

JOHN THOMAS ROCHEAD 1814-1878

Born in Edinburgh, he trained there under William Burn and David Bryce. He moved to Glasgow and became an apprentice and then Chief Draughtsman to David and James Hamilton, in 1837, along with Charles Wilson and Thomas Gildard. He established his own practice in 1841 and produced country houses, villas, tenements, terraces and commercial buildings and designed some of Glasgow's fine Gothic churches. He made his name with his competition winning design for the National Monument to William Wallace, Bridge of Allan. He moved back to Edinburgh in 1870, where he died in 1878.

WORK WITHIN THE NECROPOLIS

Hugh Cogan Monument
John Bell Monument
James Davidson of Ruchill
Dunn of Duntocher
Robert Barclay Monument
Rev Dr Thomas Brown Monument

OTHER WORK INCLUDES

The Wallace Monument, Stirling
St Vincent Street
Bank of Scotland Trongate
Bank of Scotland St Vincent Place
Northpark House, formerly BBC Scotland's headquarters.
Buckingham Terrace
Grosvenor Terrace
Ruskin Terrace

JAMES THOMSON 1835-1905

James Thomson was born in Glasgow in 1835 and was apprenticed to James Brown of Brown and Carrick around 1850 before securing a place in the office of John Baird (Primus). From around 1855 he was the main designer in Baird's practice because of Baird's mental illness and had a significant influence in the design of the Iron Building in Jamaica Street.

He became a partner in 1858, but the practice was not called Baird & Thomson until Baird died in 1859 and Thomson inherited the practice. Thomson briefly continued Baird's work in cast-iron facades and it became one of the largest practices in Scotland. He married twice and both his sons, James Baird Thomson and William Aitken Thomson, both trained in his practice and were made partners in May 1899. He died in 1905 at the age of 70.

WORK WITHIN THE NECROPOLIS

Charles Clark MacKirdy Monument
Neilson of Arnewood Monument

OTHER WORK INCLUDES

Gardner's Warehouse
Crown Circus
Victoria Terrace
Belhaven Terrace
Thomson Street School
Grand Hotel Charing Cross Glasgow
Birkwood House Lanarkshire
General David Elliot MacKirdy Monument

CHARLES RENNIE MACKINTOSH
1868-1928

Charles Rennie Mackintosh lived in Dennistoun in Firpark Terrace, overlooking the Necropolis between 1875 and 1892. At fifteen Mackintosh began evening classes at Glasgow School of Art and a year later, he joined John Hutchison's architectural practice to train as a draughtsman. In 1889 he joined the more famous firm of Honeyman & Keppie, eventually becoming a partner in 1901.

He met Margaret Macdonald, at Glasgow School of Art and they married in 1900. Her input was essential to the success of the working partnership and her influence is obvious in Mackintosh interiors.

They left Glasgow in 1913 and Mackintosh spent most of the rest of his life painting in the south of France and they both died in London.

WORK WITHIN THE NECROPOLIS

Alexander McCall Monument

OTHER WORK INCLUDES

Windyhill, Kilmacolm
The Hill House, Helensburgh
Queen's Cross Church
Scotland Street School
The Willow Tearooms
Glasgow School of Art
Glasgow Herald Offices

JAMES HAMILTON 1826-1894

The son of John Hamilton, the manager of the St. Rollox Chemical Works. James Hamilton was apprenticed to Alexander Kirkland architects in the late 1840s, during which time he designed several monuments for the Necropolis. He set up his own practice in Glasgow and Belfast after winning a competition for the Ulster Bank, Belfast in 1857. Hamilton's son became a partner in 1877 although this ended after a disagreement in 1884. 10 years later they tried again and this time the partnership ended with James Hamilton's death that same year in 1894.

WORK WITHIN THE NECROPOLIS

John Henry Alexander Monument
David Robertson Monument
Aitken of Dalmoak Mausoleum 1875

OTHER WORK INCLUDES

Tillie & Henderson's warehouse,
Ulster Bank in Sligo and Trim
Villas in and around Rothesay
Warehouse, Watson Street/Gallowgate corner
Rollox U.P. Church
Shawlands Academy

JAMES FILLANS 1808-1852

Born in Wilsontown, Lanarkshire, on 27 March 1808, he originally worked as a handloom weaver in Paisley before training as a stone mason.

Serving his apprenticeship as a stone mason with the builder Hall McLatchie, he carved the Corinthian capitals on the Glasgow Royal Exchange in Royal Exchange Square, for which he earned a the nickname: 'The Young Athenian'.

He moved to Glasgow around 1830 where he set up a studio in Miller Street and his success here enabled him to move to London in search of society patronage, during which time he impressed Sir Francis Chantrey, who recommended him to his aristocratic patrons.

Fillans produced a number of cemetery monuments, each incorporating a marble portrait bust, medallion or symbolic sculpture. He particularly admired the poet William Motherwell and eventually produced his monument for the Necropolis, spending the night before its dedication carving its details. The monument has since lost the Parian marble bust of Motherwell, and its friezes of scenes from Motherwell's life and works, Halberd The Grim etc, are badly decayed.

At the time of Fillan's death, in Glasgow in 1852, he was working on the John Henry Alexander Monument, for the Necropolis, which was completed by A H Ritchie.

WORK WITHIN THE NECROPOLIS

Dugald Moore
Dr Jacobus Brown
William Motherwell

ALEXANDER HANDYSIDE RITCHIE 1804-1870

The son of a Musselburgh brickmaker and ornamental plasterer. He attended art, architecture and anatomy classes at Edinburgh School of Arts in 1823 and then studied in Rome. He returned to Musselburgh in 1830 and opened a studio in Edinburgh, in 1842. He exhibited regularly at the RSA, RA, and was elected ARSA in 1846.

His work in Edinburgh with his brother John Ritchie, were portrait busts for patrons and statuary on Edinburgh's Central Public Library, the Royal College of Physicians, Queen Street and the Commercial Bank, George Street.

In Glasgow, he executed an Armorial Group for the former Bank of Scotland in 176 Ingram Street, the John Henry Alexander Monument, in the Glasgow Necropolis and modelled the Law Lord keystone heads for the Royal Faculty of Procurators, in West George Street.

Despite considerable artistic success and aristocratic patronage, he died in 1870, aged 66, virtually penniless leaving an estate valued at £6.10.6d.

WORK WITHIN THE NECROPOLIS

John Henry Alexander

JAMES PITTENDRIGH MACGILLIVRAY
1856-1938

Born in Inverurie, son of sculptor William Ewan Macgillivray, he trained with William Brodie from age 13, and worked with ornamental plasterer James Steel in Glasgow, on some interior decoration. He assisted John Mossman on his Campbell and Livingstone statues before becoming an independent sculptor. He was a supporter of William Morris and sculpted a bas relief of him which he travelled to London to present to him in person. He married Frieda Rohl, an established painter, who was the first treasurer of the Glasgow Society of Lady Artists in 1886.

His studio was in Bath Street and he produced portrait busts of painter, Joseph Crawhall and Thomas Carlyle and produced a number of monuments in Glasgow's cemeteries which feature bronze portraits and reliefs.

As an architectural sculptor he produced figurative work for a number of important Glasgow buildings in the 1880s which include the City Chambers. He was a painter, philosopher, musician and distinguished poet, as well as a sculptor.

After moving to Edinburgh in 1894, he produced many busts and medallions for Edinburgh patrons and also produced a report for the Scottish Education Department, which contributed to the establishment of Edinburgh College of Art and which included the layout of the building. He became Sculptor Royal in 1921 and died in 1938 aged 82.

WORK WITHIN THE NECROPOLIS

Peter Stewart
Alexander McCall
Allan Family

ARCHIBALD MACFARLANE SHANNAN
1850-1915

Educated at Glasgow University, he was apprenticed to his father, the builder Peter Shannan, and began work as an architect. He was responsible for construction of buildings in the Cameroons, West Africa, and in Texas, USA before taking up sculpture.

After training and studying in Paris, he returned to Glasgow and established a successful career producing portrait busts, public monuments and architectural sculpture. He produced several bronze medallions of local academics and clerics. These include the seated statues of Mrs Isabella Elder, in Elder Park, Govan and Lord Kelvin in Kelvingrove Park.

During World War II, three of Shannan's important works were destroyed. These were the bronze figures representing Immortality (or Glory), Fame and Success for Kelvingrove Art Gallery, whose removal was deemed necessary as an air raid precaution in 1940. These 'Glasgow-style' figures were cut down on the orders of the museum's Director, T.J. Honeyman, and later scrapped. In 1999, in an article by Gary Nisbet: The Art of Success, 10 April, 1999, a call was made to have copies or modern replacements for the statues included as part of the proposed restoration of the building but this was rejected as inappropriate. Shannan was injured in an accident and died in 1915 aged 65. He was buried in the Southern Necropolis where his headstone is toppled and covered with moss.

WORK WITHIN THE NECROPOLIS

George Mason

J AND G MOSSMAN

This family firm of monumental and architectural sculptors was established in 1857, by the brothers John Mossman, George Mossman and William Mossman II, after training with and succeeding their father, William Mossman I, at his sculpture studios in 83 North Frederick Street, Glasgow. They produced a huge number of monuments for the Glasgow Necropolis and other cemeteries throughout the country.

These were often carved to the designs of some of Glasgow's finest architects, but most were chosen from the Mossmans' own designs.

In 2005 they restored the Alexander McCall Monument in the Glasgow Necropolis free of charge. This Iona Cross was designed by C R Mackintosh and sculpted by J & G Mossman in 1888 but was broken by vandals in 2004. J & G Mossman Ltd's head office is currently based in Alloa, Clackmannanshire, but they continue to operate a showroom in the High Street, Glasgow.

WORK WITHIN THE NECROPOLIS

Peter Lawrence
Thomas Gildard
Mary Anne Lockhart
and many others

CLUBB AND MCLEAN

A prolific firm of monumental sculptors established by Alexander Clubb and his cousin, Peter McLean, as Clubb & McLean, in 1853 but they occasionally signed their work McLean & Clubb or individually.

Sculptor Alexander Clubb was born near Dunoon in 1806, and lived in Glasgow in Springburn, with his wife and son, Alexander.

Peter McLean was born in Springburn in 1837, the son of sculptor Alexander McLean whose workshop was in Kirk Lane and he succeeded to it after his father's death.

Working in sandstone, the firm produced a significant number of impressive sculptural monuments for the Glasgow Necropolis and Glasgow's other cemeteries, and, like Mossman, often to the designs of the well known architects of the time.

WORK WITHIN THE NECROPOLIS

Robert Stewart
David Robertson
William Harper Minnoch
James and David Laurie

THOMAS EDINGTON & SONS
1804-1903
also known as THE PHOENIX FOUNDRY

One of Glasgow's oldest iron foundries was established by Thomas Edington in Queen Street.

WORKS WITHIN THE NECROPOLIS INCLUDE

Gates to the Jews' Enclosure 1832
Designed by John Park of Anderston

Necropolis Main Gates 1838
Designed by David Hamilton

OTHER WORKS

Phoenix Park Fountain 1891 which stood in Phoenix Park, Cowcaddens. The park was named after the foundry. The fountain became delerict and was demolished in 1959.

Edington's son, James Edington, was involved with the Eagle Foundry in Port Dundas.

WALTER MACFARLANE & CO
1850-1965
also known as the SARACEN FOUNDRY

The company was established in Glasgow by Walter Macfarlane, with partners Thomas Russell and James Marshall, in Dovehill, behind the Saracen Head Inn, in the Gallowgate hence the name. They moved to premises in Washington Street and finally James Boucher designed their Possilpark foundry which was a showcase for their products, complete with a huge glass and iron dome and elaborate decorative castings on its gateway - the site covered 12 acres. Macfarlane created the suburb of Possilpark to house the firm's workforce.

Macfarlane's nephew also Walter was adopted as his son, Walter Macfarlane II. He became a partner and succeeded to the firm on his uncle's death in 1885. He commissioned architects James Salmon and J Gaff Gillespie to redesign some of the interiors of the family home at 22 Park Circus, (now Glasgow's Registry Office).

The foundry specialised in drinking fountains, bandstands, lamp standards, pre-fabricated buildings and architectural features and was known for its quality and elegance mass-producing designs by architects such as James Sellars, John Burnet and Alexander 'Greek' Thomson.

INDEX OF MONUMENTS

153

SELECT BIBLIOGRAPHY

A selection of published sources :

Glasgow Through a Looking Glass
by Douglas N Anderson 1982

The Wee Green Book by Neil Baxter 2007

The Glasgow Necropolis Heritage Trail and Historical
Account by James J Berry BA (Hons) 1985

The Glasgow Graveyard Guide by Jimmy Black 1992

Biographic and Descriptive Sketches of Glasgow
Necropolis by George Blair 1857

Hand Heart and Soul by Elizabeth Cummings 2006

Glasgow by David Daiches 1982

The Songs of Scotland, adapted to their appropriate
melodies, by George Farquhar Graham 1853

Tea and Taste by Perilla Kinchin 1991

The Hidden History of Glasgow's Women - The THENEW
FACTOR by Elspeth King 1993

The People's Palace and Glasgow Green
by Elspeth King 1991

Rambles Round Glasgow by Hugh MacDonald 1854

Public Sculpture of Glasgow by Ray McKenzie 2002

The Merchants' House of Glasgow 1605 - 2005
by Susan Milligan 2004

The Clyde - A Portrait of a River by Michael Moss 1997

Glasgow in 1901 - by James Hamilton Muir
Reprint and introduction by Perilla Kinchen 2001

The People's Palace Book editor Mark O'Neill 1998

Death by Design by Ronnie Scott 2005

Language of Flowers by Margaret Pickston 1968

Necropolis Glasguensis with Observation on Ancient
and Modern Tombs and Sepulture by John Strang 1831

The Old Glasgow Club 75th Anniversary 1975

A Glasgow Keek Show by Frank Wordsall 1981